Concrete Steps

Concrete Steps

Coming of Age
in a Once-Big City

LARRY C. KERPELMAN

PB

Pratt Brook Communications, LLC
ACTON, MASSACHUSETTS

Concrete Steps: Coming of Age in a Once-Big City
Larry C. Kerpelman

ISBN: 978-1-942545-48-4
LCCN: 2016936889
Copyright © 2016 Larry C. Kerpelman
All rights reserved.

Pratt Brook Communications, LLC
ACTON, MASSACHUSETTS
An imprint of Wyatt-MacKenzie

For my children, Todd and Janna,
you give me hope. *L'Tikvah.*

To the memory of my parents, Morris and Fannie,
they gave me life. *L'Chaim.*

"And without the past, . . . it becomes harder for us to understand who we are now, and where we might be going. To carry the past comfortably is to be whole."

— Howard Axelrod, "In Search of Lost Time,"
Boston Sunday Globe

CONTENTS

PREFACE

THIS IS THE STORY of the youth I left behind in 1958 and my struggle for the independence that enabled me to leave it behind. This is the story, too, of a particular place (Baltimore, Maryland) at a particular time (the 1940s and '50s), in a particular neighborhood (though it had no name then—it was just where we lived—it's now called "Woodbrook"), and in a particular family. It's a story of a boy coming of age in the Jewish quarter of a then-large American city during and after World War II. It's a story of a young boy playing, learning, questioning, rebelling (mildly), maturing (somewhat). This story is unique in that it's *my* story—how I grew up in *my* family and in *my* neighborhood, developed *my* attitudes and values, and got to go out on *my* own.

In other ways, though, it is a story that many other boys in similar circumstances who came of age in big cities during that period could tell. Boys—now men—whose lives, like mine, overlapped Franklin D. Roosevelt's and Al Capone's, Babe Ruth's and Adolph Hitler's, Clark Gable's and Sigmund Freud's. Boys who grew up in a world where a single telephone—and a rotary dial one at that—and a single car served an entire family, if they were fortunate enough to afford even those. Boys who had to find their way tentatively because their parents were newcomers to a country in which they were a distinct minority. Boys who lived in an extraordinary time in history.

Life in the 21st century is different from what it was in the middle of the 20th. So much has been lost—some good, some bad—in the period between then and now. Life as it's lived currently is not how life has always been lived, and I want to give a flavor of that life—through my life—to readers who may want to explore it and care to understand it. What historian William Cronon wrote about examining world or national history applies equally, I believe, to examining personal and cultural history. In his book *Changes in the Land*, he wrote:

> . . . when we probe beneath the familiar surfaces of the present, peeling away one by one the layers of our own memories and the accumulated strata of the historical record, we almost always discover changes so profound that we scarcely recognize what we are seeing. . . . People lived differently back then, thought differently, and conceived of their place in the universe in ways so different from our own that it can take an immense imaginative effort to understand them on their own terms. And yet, just as strikingly, it was they, those people in the past, who laid the foundations for the lives we now lead and the world we now inhabit. Asking how so alien a Then could have become so familiar a Now is a never-failing source of wonder that can transform the way we think, not just about the world, but about ourselves as well.

Growing up amid the concrete steps, sidewalks, streets, and urban hubbub of a sizable American city in the 1940s and 1950s had its highs and lows. Looking back, I feel on the whole privileged to have lived the kind of youth I did with the kind of upbringing I had. It was not an economically advantaged youth, but it was an experientially rich one. Where other people have been sheltered from contact and confrontation with people of other races and cultures, I was exposed to them in a way that was natural. Where some have heard about the immigrant lifestyle, I grew up within it.

I have relied on my memory of events and dialogue, of course, for what I wrote in this memoir. But also I have been fortunate to have read and heard of other episodes and events through letters from, writings by, and conversations with members of my family and friends of my family that I have preserved. Friends and relatives may remember my story and the scenes I describe differently. Everyone has his or her own perception of reality; this is my recollection of my reality as I lived it and remember it.

Here and there throughout what follows I have changed the name of a person or the details of a place in order to spare someone discomfort or embarrassment. A few of the places I refer to—their names and even their physical attributes—have changed since that now-long ago time. Some may not even exist anymore. Half a century is more than half a lifetime, after all.

Much else has changed since that time in the city where I grew up, Baltimore, Maryland. In the 1940s, it was the seventh-largest city in the U.S., a gritty, busy manufacturing and shipping port with a population of 859,100. Most recently, the 2010 U.S. Census pegged Baltimore's population at 620,961, ranking it 21st in size in the country. Even considering the city plus its environs—for those statistics sticklers among you—it now ranks 20th in size among U.S. Metropolitan Statistical Areas. How the mighty have fallen.

A couple of caveats before we go further. First, some readers may note that the occasional Hebrew words in this book are not rendered in modern Hebrew (the language adopted by the

State of Israel after it became an independent nation in 1948). I use, instead, the Hebrew I learned when I was coming of age before the founding of that nation, the older style that, for the most part, uses an "s" sound where modern Hebrew has a "t" sound.

Second, the long-ago time that is the focus of this book was less politically correct than the present time, yet I have chosen to include some indelicate thoughts and terms just the same, thoughts and terms that might make some readers squirm. I do it to keep the scenes as real as they were then, and to avoid using euphemisms that will make the circumstances and situations I describe sound artificial. This is how people talked and thought back then. In many respects society has changed for the better, but I think I owe it to you, the reader, to give the full flavor of that world back then, with all its bruises and blemishes.

1

TO BEGIN AT THE END

"Expatriates always think about their life
up to the point of departure."

— Jill Ker Conway, "Points of Departure,"
in *Inventing the Truth: The Art and Craft of Memoir*

WE STOOD AT THE SIDE of the road, my father and I,
the entrance ramp to the highway leading north 100
yards ahead of us, the family home, eight miles behind us. Cars
whooshed by, oblivious to the personal drama playing out at
the road's edge. I was about to embark on a new phase of my
life, and Dad, as always, found it hard to say goodbye. He had
insisted on following me in his car after I left home in my car
until I reached the highway that headed north, to say our goodbyes there. And now we were there, and now we were to say
goodbye, and now I was to start on the next phase of my life.

The year was 1958, I was 19, and I was heading off to
begin graduate school at The University of Rochester, a seven-
hour drive from Baltimore. The 10-year-old, green, stick-shift
Plymouth my parents had owned and had recently given me to
take to graduate school—the "machine," they always called

it—was filled with my clothes and other possessions. Important among them were the books in psychology I had used in college, the information about the graduate program in psychology I was about to embark on, and details of the motel I had arranged to live in while I looked for permanent lodging in a town I knew next to nothing about.

Dad hugged me, and I hugged him, that bear of a man, and he told me he loved me—that I was a good son. He advised me to "write home, at least once a week, even if it's only a postcard," adding "for your mother's sake." I had said my goodbyes to Mom at home. When I left her standing at the front door, there were tears in her eyes, and her short, round frame looked even smaller than usual to me as I looked back. I suspect, too, when I pulled onto the highway to head north, that Dad had a tear or two in his eyes.

In the year before this, I had spent much of my energy plotting a course that would bring me to this place along the highway. I was declaring my independence from my parents and embarking on a life course that they did not fully understand and only reluctantly believed I should take. I was leaving behind the city in which I was born and raised, and the family within whose embrace I had grown to almost-adulthood. I was the first of my parents' five children to leave home before being married.

With that parting at the edge of the highway, I was leaving the family that nurtured me, the parents that raised me, the extended family that surrounded me, the neighborhood that socialized me, the war that influenced me, the schools that educated me, the games that entertained me, the sports that challenged me, the jobs that disciplined me, the music that thrilled me, the religion that acculturated me, and the girls that charmed me.

Once on the highway, I watched in the rearview mirror as all that faded away behind me. With the attitude of invulnerability that is the gift of youth (and sometimes its bane), I saw ahead of me nothing but a lifetime of positive experiences, some adventure, and a chance, finally, to strike out on my own. Although I have since visited both my home city and my family home often, I have never returned to either for a stay of any length. I was, it was to turn out, taking concrete steps on the path toward being my own person.

2

In the Bosom of My Family

"The tale of someone's life begins before they are born."
— Michael Wood, *Shakespeare*

TO BEGIN AT THE very beginning, I was born mid-afternoon on January 27, 1939, in Sinai Hospital in Baltimore. The hospital at that time was located on Monument Street, just around the corner from world-renowned Johns Hopkins Hospital. Dr. Max Koppelman, a distant family relative, officiated at my birth. Among immigrant families—even today—where finances were tight, friends, relatives, and connections were often used to obtain services for less than they might cost in the "outside world," and thus it was that a distant cousin delivered me.

Family lore has it that although my mother began to feel labor pains early that day, a Friday, she felt obligated to scrub the floors and finish making the gefilte fish for the family, as she always did to usher in the Jewish Sabbath that evening, before she allowed herself to go to the hospital. Not part of family lore—because my parents always tried to shield their children from the embarrassing and the unpleasant—was the fact that most likely my appearance on the scene was an accident. There were already four children in the family, all born within two or three years of one another. By the time I was born, Leonard was 14, Billy was 11, Margie was nine, and Charlie was six. My advent after a gap of six years, then, was very likely an unplanned one. Further evidence for this supposition is that the hand-me-downs that were given to me to wear as I grew up were from my cousins, not my brothers (as their hand-me-downs were). I think my mother did not save Charlie's clothes to hand down because she did not expect to have more children to hand them down to.

My parents named me Larry Cyril. My first name was inscribed on my birth certificate as Larry because Mom did not want to provide an opportunity for other kids to tease me with "Hey, Lawrence" this and "Oh, Lawrence" that, delivered in that snippy tone children often adopt. I now wish my parents had given me the more formal name of Lawrence, as Larry on a diploma or as the author of a publication looks so—well—informal and strange. My Hebrew name was Lazar, to honor my maternal grandfather's brother of that name. My middle name of Cyril was to honor another deceased relative, my mother's aunt, Tsippe Maria. Growing up, I was so embarrassed by the unusual name Cyril that I kept it hidden from anyone I came in contact with.

At a few days old, I was brought home from the hospital. Margie delights to this day in telling me, "When I saw you for the first time, you were the most beautiful child I had ever seen; you had such beautiful baby blue eyes." I doubt whether anyone now would describe me so effusively.

The home I was brought to was a three-story red brick row house built in 1915 at 3506 Holmes Avenue in Baltimore. It sat cheek by jowl with the other row houses it was attached to, each house an exact carbon copy inside and out of the others on the two blocks that made up Holmes Avenue in the northwest quadrant of the city. At the front of each house was a small concrete porch, with concrete steps leading down from it to the cement sidewalk at street level. The front of each house had a postage-stamp-size "lawn," which it later fell on me to mow with a push mower. While it wasn't much, the lawn did provide a patch of green in front of the house, making it superior in my mind to other row houses located farther in toward downtown Baltimore: Those row houses had front steps landing directly onto the pavement with no grass near them at all. In the rear of each house on our block was a slightly larger back yard and one-car garage accessed via the alley in back. There, in that neighborhood of attached row houses inhabited mostly by first-generation Jewish-American families, I began my life and lived my youth. There, among the concrete steps, sidewalks, and streets of Baltimore, I received my education, established my friendships, and learned my values. There, my story really begins.

The family census now reaching seven with my birth, we all fit, after a fashion, into the eight rooms on the first two floors of our row house—entry hallway, living room, dining room, den, and kitchen on the first floor, and, on the second floor, four bedrooms and our sole bathroom. That sole bathroom—with its floor of small hexagonal white tiles, enamel-coated sink basin supported by two metal posts, toilet, and enamel-coated clawfoot bathtub with a jerry-rigged shower connected to the faucet by a flexible tube—was the scene of pandemonium every weekday morning as the four boys in the family crowded into it, in twos, to wash, shower, shave, and take care of their bodily functions, all in time to get to school or work. Suffering from insomnia as he did, Dad was usually in and out of the bathroom most mornings before his children even awoke. Mom tried to sleep late. We reluctantly vacated the little loo room for Margie so she could do her morning thing, but she had to hurry along and not dawdle "doing her hair" if she wanted to avoid the wrath and knocks on the door of her brothers waiting to get in. Somehow, we all managed to get through the mornings using that little bathroom without inflicting serious injury upon one another.

In the dank, gray stone cellar of the house was a wringer washing machine, a steel tub on wheels with an agitator inside that sloshed the clothes clean. It stood next to a utilitarian concrete double sink, one side of the sink used for soaking the clothes before being dumped into the washer—there to be attacked by the agitator—the other to rinse them in after being taken from the washer. After Mom washed and rinsed the clothes, she did not transfer them to a dryer. Although there were such things back then, no one we knew had one. Rather, Mom cranked the wet clothes through the wringer and then finished drying them on clotheslines in the back yard, winter—when they would sometimes freeze stiff—or summer—when they always dried quickly and smelled of the outdoors. Once they were dry, she took to ironing the clothes, sprinkling each item first with water from an old soda bottle topped by a stopper with holes in it. Permanent press clothing was years into the future.

The cellar also held a monster oil-fired furnace that had once burned coal. My brothers remembered when the coal furnace ashes had to be emptied periodically, but it had later been converted to an oil-fired furnace, so ash dumping was a thing of the past by the time I came along. The cellar still retained the separate coal storage room in it, however, where in earlier times a truck would deliver its load of coal via a chute through the coal room window, there to await its fate of being shoveled into our furnace to be burned. Some of the houses on our block still burned coal and received their coal deliveries that way. I used to like watching the coal trucks back up to those houses, tip their load onto a chute that went into their basement window, and hear the coal rattle down it through the window and into the basement, a gray cloud of coal dust rising ominously over the scene.

There was a third floor in our brick row house, but it was not ours to use. To bring in extra income—for every dollar counted—my parents wedged in a tiny kitchen, an even tinier bathroom, and a bed-sitting room up there to create an apartment they could rent out. They could not wedge in a separate entrance, though, in this narrow row house, so at any time of the day or night, people who weren't part of my family, our tenants, would walk in through the sole front door of our house to go up the only staircase to reach their third floor apartment. Their unannounced presence in our midst never seemed strange to them or us, nor did the fact that they had a key to our house. That's just the way it was when you rented out the top floor of your house. My mother had a knack for picking out and ingratiating tenants so that they and our family were cordial to one another, for the most part. Aside from the occasional drinker or deadbeat, our tenants presented no problem to us.

I shared a bedroom—and a lot of my growing up—with my brother Charlie. That second-floor bedroom was just big enough for our two brown-painted metal-frame twin beds with a narrow space in between. There was a closet in the corner, wallpaper with little red and green flowers on a white back-ground, a steam radiator painted silver, and a window covered by wooden-slatted venetian blinds. On the other side of that bedroom—with a white-curtained French door in between—was the bedroom Billy and Leonard shared, similar in size and layout to Charlie's and my bedroom. Margie, being the only girl, had a bedroom all her own down the hall and was envied by us boys because of that. The fourth bedroom, also on the second floor, was my parents'. Off that bedroom was a screened tenement-type porch. In Baltimore's hot and insufferably humid summers, the children of our family would set up camp cots of canvas stretched across wooden frames on the screened porch to catch the slight breeze that might make sleep for the night possible

———————

Both my father, Morris, and mother, Fannie, came to the United States as children from greater Russia in the early part of the 20th century, a few years before the Bolshevik Revolution and World War I. They were part of the large migration of two-and-a-half million Jews from Eastern Europe to the United States between the latter part of the 19th century and the early part of the 20th. Dad's family came from Khodorkov, in the Skvirsky district, or county, of Kiev province, about 60 miles west-south-west of the city of Kiev in what is now Ukraine. In 1912, when Dad was 11, he came to the U.S. with his parents and seven of their eight children. As an infant, Mom and two siblings—an older sister and a younger brother—came across with their mother in the early years of the 20th century from Dvinsk (now called Daugavpils) in Latvia. There had been a fourth child who died shortly after birth. Mom's father, my maternal grand-father, had already come to the U.S. a year or so earlier to establish a foothold and earn the money that would enable him to send for the rest of his family. In the ensuing years in the U.S., seven more children were born into my mother's family.

They all came to the U.S. for the same reason millions of immigrants before, and millions since, came—for the educational, economic, and social opportunities denied them in their old country. For my grandparents and parents, it was especially the educational opportunities their adopted country offered that they most sought. They came, too, to escape the persecution, restrictions, and violence visited upon them by the majority population that have been the lot of Jewish people through the millennia.

The Holocaust Museum in Washington, D.C., has an enclosed bridge connecting two of its buildings. On the bridge walls are etched the names of the numerous *shtetls* (villages) and towns in which the Jewish populations were annihilated during World War II by the Germans—often with the enthusiastic cooperation of the local non-Jewish population. Both Khodorkov and Dvinsk are etched on that wall.

My father, Morris, was a sturdily-built, strong man, almost six feet in height, with a cleft chin and, for most of the time I was growing up, a mustache. All that combined to move many, many people to declare that he bore a remarkable resemblance to the actor Clark Gable. He also had, for most of that time, a two-and-a-half pack a day cigarette habit. He always had a cigarette dangling from his mouth and always smelled of cigarettes, and our house did, too, from both his smoke and the always full ash trays around the house. He had a wicked cigarette cough, as well. Mom was frequently after him to give up the habit. He wanted to—considered it a filthy habit—but he couldn't kick his addiction easily. Finally, in his late 50s, after one unsuccessful attempt, he succeeded in doing so.

Strong man that he was, his cigarette habit of many decades did not ultimately seem to affect his longevity, as he lived into his late 80s. My mother lasted for two years after his death in 1989, declining rapidly once he was gone. About the only positive to be garnered from my father's cigarette addiction is that it served as a negative role model, for four of his five children did not take up cigarette smoking. I'll admit I tried it a couple of times—without inhaling—but couldn't seem to find the joy in it. I also felt that the human body is a wondrous thing and that any highs it feels should be those that come naturally. For that reason, I never took up smoking or, for that matter, illicit drugs. I've even always resisted taking prescription drugs unless absolutely necessary. Mild confession here: as an adult, I do drink wine and the occasional harder spirits, but my constitution is such that I am easily overwhelmed by one or two drinks and know enough to stop—or else I fall asleep from their effects and therefore come to a "natural" stop.

Dad, like his father before him, was very gentle, and just the thought of violence scared him. But when aroused, he would seethe with an anger that visibly frightened him. On a few occasions he recounted to me, with a mix of fear and distaste, tales of conflicts with anti-Semites as he was growing up—name-calling, bullying, fights. Another time that I recall, a radio announcer spoke of a "sudden death" playoff in a sporting event we were listening to. Visibly upset upon hearing this term, Dad complained at length, "Why do they use such a term 'sudden death'? That's terrible. 'Sudden death'!" I came to believe later (psychologist that I turned out to be) that this dynamic exemplified what psychodynamic theorists call a "reaction formation," a way of reacting to unacceptable emotions by forming a behavioral disposition exactly and extremely the opposite of the fraught emotion.

Reaction formation or not, Dad was an affectionate father, attentive and solicitous whenever he was around. Unfortunately, he wasn't around all that much. From the time he came to this country as a boy of 11, he worked hard to support his family—as a newsboy, as a pin setter in a bowling alley, at whatever other jobs he could garner throughout high school. After graduating from Baltimore City College, he went on to the University of Maryland Law School, where he met and courted my mother, Fannie Kurland. Both my mother and father graduated from there, Mom being one of the first three women to receive a diploma from that law school.

A word of explanation about terminology and names is called for here. Baltimore City College (which I also attended) was, and still is, a high school (one of the oldest public high schools in the country). The University of Maryland's Law School at that time was not a post-graduate professional school as it now is but a program students attended after high school, just as they might attend an undergraduate college today.

Although my parents practiced law together for a brief period after graduating from law school, Mom soon turned her attention a short while after they married to raising their children, who began to come along quickly and regularly. Dad went into business with his brother, Al. Dad had to work hard to keep the Atlas Upholstered Furniture Company, his small business at 21 North High Street, going when Al left it precipitately after it almost went under during the Great Depression. As a result, my father usually remained hard at work at Atlas Upholstered Furniture Company until late each evening. Even so, when he did get home, Dad was always ready to take us kids to Moe's candy store when we greeted him at the door with pleas of "Take us to Moe's! Take us to Moe's!" I don't think he ever refused, as tired as he often must have been after long hours of trying to make a go of the business. He struggled for a number of years to keep that small business going, but ultimately, in the 1950s, it folded. When it did, he took a job selling furniture at Sears, and Mom went back to work—after a hiatus of many years raising their children—as a secretary to the head of the Sociology Department at the newly founded Baltimore County campus of the University of Maryland.

Mom was the driving force in the household, by virtue of her own background and take-charge personality and my father's absence from the picture for much of the time. As the second oldest girl in her family, much of the rearing of her younger siblings in her own large family had fallen on her shoulders, as her older sister, Helen, was quite career-oriented and had little time to tend to her younger sisters and brothers. My mother was fierce when it came to matters of family. You knew she would take on anyone in defense of her children or to further their progress in life. Fair of face, short, and tending toward stoutness, Mom was strong-willed, as she had to be to survive her tough life and to take charge of her younger siblings, and she pretty much directed all my decisions. Once I reached adolescence, however, calling on resources I was not aware I had, I began the struggle to be my own person.

Mom was known far and wide for her propensity to take in people. Whoever came to our home was invited to stay for a snack, for lunch, for supper, for a night, for two nights, for a few months—whatever they needed and wanted. Various aunts, uncles, cousins, and other "relatives" whose linkage to our family were a mystery to me as a child were often at our house, coming to gossip, reminisce, *kvell* (express extraordinary pride), or whatever moved them. One frequent visitor was "Cousin Sophie" Samler, a widow whose relation to us I could never quite disentangle. Sophie had a thick eastern European accent, and we referred to her as the *grine kuzine* (greenhorn cousin). Another frequent visitor to our house was Uncle Ike Pearl, my mother's uncle and therefore my great uncle. His wife, Tsippe Maria, had died before I was born, and when Uncle Ike visited us, his talk would often circle around to her, whereupon he would ultimately dissolve into tears. Since Jews of my generation were traditionally named after a deceased relative, my middle name, Cyril (Tsiril in Hebrew), derives in a roundabout fashion from the name of Ike's wife, Tsippe. Uncle Ike was given a prominent place in our household whenever he visited.

My mother always put up relatives who visited from out of town even though we didn't have a guest bedroom for them to sleep in. She offered them my bed, as the youngest, to sleep in, telling them, "Larry can always sleep on the cot," one of the fold-up canvas camp cots we hauled out for occasions like this.

Mom never asked me if I'd mind giving up my bed, and the guests who took it over seldom thanked me, either. It just seemed to everyone to be the expected order of things. When we didn't have enough cots, Mom spread out cotton comforters on the floor for members of our family (and at times some of the visiting guests themselves) to sleep on. Sometimes the invitations to stay were so last-minute that if my siblings were out for an evening and guests showed up, Mom took to leaving a note on the telephone table telling everyone where to sleep. Our small house was populated so often with so many visiting relatives, along with friends of my sister and brothers, that one returning guest, a friend of one of my brothers, brought us a gift of a set of paper napkins imprinted with the words "Kerpelman Hotel."

For an extended period, my cousin Dorothy lived with us, too. The younger child of my mother's older sister, Helen, Dorothy was mildly intellectually disabled, and Helen, whose focus was always on getting ahead professionally and socially, did not have time to devote to raising her intellectually disabled daughter. So, of course, Mom took Dorothy in, and she lived in our house during my early school years. Similarly, my Aunt Katie (Mom's sister) and her husband Bob lived in the apartment above us for a while in the early years of their marriage.

A good Jewish mother, Mom was always after me to eat because she considered me to be skinny. It's true, I was not the kind of pudgy child Jewish mothers liked to see. On top of that, I was a picky eater. And on top of that, I didn't particularly like my mother's cooking. Dad liked her cooking and literally ate it up—the boiled brisket, boiled chicken, chicken soup, *kasha*, *lukshen kugel*, and *tsimmis* she typically cooked. To my taste, however, old-country Jewish cooking of the type my mother engaged in was insipid. Its underlying principle seemed to me to be to use spices that cancelled one another out so that the food ended up tasting bland, and then to cook it to death to ensure that whatever flavor remained was cooked out of it.

Mom was so happy whenever I *would* eat a particular food, she pushed that food at me at every opportunity. I liked plain butter, straight (strange as that may seem), so she would leave pats of it in a little glass dish on the kitchen table for me to eat. When she made tuna fish salad and saw that I picked out the celery to eat but left the tuna fish, she was just as happy to make more tuna fish salad so that I would at least eat the celery in it. When my parents saw that I liked Hydrox cookies, they made sure to keep a constant supply of them in the house.

When I was in grade school, on special occasions Mom (sometimes joined by Dad) would take me for a treat to one or another of my favorite restaurants. These were not fancy places, just local restaurants whose food I did like. Wilson's Restaurant, on Pennsylvania Avenue, was a favorite of both hers and mine. Their crab soup was the best in the city (second to Dad's), we thought, made just so with decent size chunks of crab in it. My favorite entrée there was imperial crab, essentially a lazy-man's crab where crab meat picked from steamed crabs was placed in a crab shell or large clam shell, sprinkled lightly with bread crumbs, and then baked. Another favorite place of mine was the White Coffee Pot Restaurant, at North and Linden Avenues. Often if I were going out somewhere with my parents, they would take me to the White Coffee Pot first, where I would invariably order the breaded veal cutlet smothered in gravy, served with mashed potatoes covered with more gravy, and string beans.

Once her children began to appear with some regularity, my mother took actions not to be overwhelmed by the demands of the five children as we grew up. She insisted that each of us learn enough of the basics of cooking that we could at least survive on our own if we had to. While no great cook herself, she taught all of us the rudiments of kitchen utensil use, basic cooking techniques, and throwing a meal together. We all prepared our own breakfasts, allowing her to sleep later than she otherwise would if she had to get up early to feed five growing children. Dad, who suffered from insomnia, was often up before the kids awakened, and he always delighted in helping us make breakfast or making breakfast for us himself before he left for work.

As soon as we reached the appropriate age, Mom also taught her children the basic elements of selecting our clothing to wear each day so that she would not have to hop from one child to the other each morning to ensure that we were passably dressed. She taught us the rudiments of sewing so we could patch the rips in our clothing or holes in our socks that were the result of everyday living without her having to do it for us. She was firm in the belief that we should all learn how to swim so that if we found ourselves alone in the water, we'd be able to survive. My swimming lessons came more from my brother, Charlie, who was a lifeguard in his teens, than my mother, but she was the driving force behind them.

Mom was adamant, too, that all of her children learn to type, as she felt that it was something we would use no matter what work we ended up doing. She sent all of us to Strayer's Business School in downtown Baltimore to learn typing, and it served us well in our various careers. Given how excruciating it is for me to write longhand, this book (and all my other written creations) might not have seen the light of day had it not been for those typing lessons.

And my mother also introduced me to the joys and delights of the library. Despite how busy she was taking care of the household, she took me many times to the stately building that housed the central location of the Enoch Pratt Free Library on the fringes of downtown Baltimore to show me the world of books that I could explore there. I was awed by the hush of the central reading room there with its rows of tables and the almost unlimited variety of books I could ask for.

Dad, for his part, taught me how to ride a bike. He could not teach me in our neighborhood, as the only level street was Westbury Avenue, and its traffic, although light, interfered with steady bicycle practice. Instead, on weekends, he would load my older brothers' bike—a heavy, no-gears Columbia mammoth with fat balloon tires—into the family car, and we would drive to the Druid Hill Park reservoir, which had a paved, pedestrian-only road around its perimeter. There, overlooking a lovely section of the city, I would pedal the bike while Dad ran alongside it holding the rear fender to ensure I did not take a spill. Eventually, I could handle it on my own, and Dad could release his grip, catch his breath, and let me cycle on by myself.

As with so many of my peers, I was eager to learn to drive when I reached the age of 16. Although not a great driver herself, Mom taught me how to drive their '48 stick-shift green Plymouth, the one my parents later gave me to take to graduate school. But she could not park worth a damn, so it fell to my father to teach me parallel parking. We'd find a quiet street, he'd set up some waste cans we had taken with us to place in the street, and he'd teach me how to maneuver to park between them.

Like many people in that era of conformity and repression of the 1940s and '50s, Mom and Dad repressed unpleasant or "embarrassing" thoughts and occurrences. Neither of them was capable of entertaining that the circumstance of my conception was an accident, neither of them ever talked to me about sex, and many unpleasant things that happened to them were simply never talked about in front of their children. The repression that is a major part of reaction formation operated in my mother's personality as well as my father's.

Everyone wants perfect parents, but who among us have them—and who among us are them? Though they had their faults, my mother and father were the best parents they knew how to be, formed by what life put them through. And it put them through a lot: Having to learn a new language and living skills as children; raising a brood of five children themselves, the first of whom, Leonard, was seriously ill early on; dealing with the tremendous expenses of Leonard's polio treatment and rehabilitation; trying to make a living during and after the Great Depression by running an always-faltering small business, one that ultimately went belly-up in the 1950s when it could not sustain the family; and, as any parents did, having to understand and cope with changing social mores and changing times. They raised children who weren't perfect, either. But each of us in the family did the best we could with the hand we were dealt, and the foundation of whatever strengths and successes we possessed had to have come from our parents.

———•·•———

Because we shared a bedroom, because—even though six years my senior—he was the sibling closest to me in age, and because he didn't get married and leave home until he was 20 (and I was 14), Charlie was the sibling I had the longest and closest relationship with as I was growing up. He was also the sibling I most resembled. People would often remark, on seeing us two freckle-faced brothers together, how close the family resemblance was. Both Charlie and I were pleased to be compared to one another.

On weekends, when I'd wake up in the bedroom we shared on the second floor, Charlie would spirit me downstairs before I could make enough noise to awaken the rest of the family or the tenants above us on the third floor. There in our living room on weekend mornings, he and I would engage in the "Saturday Morning Fights," just as we had heard the Friday Night Fights broadcast on the radio each week.

I was enamored of the "sweet science" of boxing from my earliest days. I can't explain how a skinny kid who hated to be in a fight—on those rare occasions when I couldn't avoid one— became a fight fan. All I know is that I listened to the Friday night fights on the radio avidly every week. From Madison Square Garden, the bout of the evening was brought to a vast listening public, of which I was a regular, by Gillette razors and blades ("Look Sharp! Feel Sharp! Be Sharp!" its commercials chanted) and announced by Don Dunphy. Although I never could see any of those fights that were broadcast on the radio, I vividly imagined how Kid Gavilan, my favorite fighter of all time, threw his trademark bolo punch; I could describe each of Joe Louis's many knockouts; and I could describe Carmen Basilio's impressive physique perfectly to you—all from the detailed "blow-by-blow", as it was called, that Don Dunphy delivered on the radio every Friday night. Naturally, listening to them on the radio, I did not imagine the reality of the blood and brutality of the fights, something that was only revealed to me some years later when we acquired a television set.

I had a running series of wagers on the outcomes of the Friday night fights with our neighbor from across the street, Warren Komins. Each week we bet a quarter on the outcome of the fight. We never collected from each other, instead keeping a running tab in our heads of who owed who what amount. We kept this going for well over a year. At this late date, if one of us decides to collect on the betting debt, the interest charges would be astronomical.

For those morning bouts with my brother we wore boxing gloves our Uncle Eddie had given us that once belonged to a boxer he had managed. In our Saturday morning fights, not only was Charlie the Carmen Basilio to my Kid Gavilan, he also did double duty as announcer Don Dunphy. Blow-by-blow, thrust-by-thrust, Carmen-Don-Charlie boxed and announced, announced and boxed.

"The Kid edges into Basilio! He gives him a left, then a right, and now he steps away to deliver his famous bolo punch. Basilio is rocked, ladies and gentlemen!"

Now, instead of using my imagination to see the Friday night fights, I was actually in the Saturday morning fights! Funny, try as he might, Charlie always lost somehow, so at the end of every event, he lifted my scrawny gloved right arm and pronounced me "The winner and still 'champeen.'"

My most vivid memory of those events, however, was not my winning—unbelievably—every match, but the bout where I got carried away, surprised the hell out of both Charlie and myself, landed a hard punch on his nose, and started it bleeding. Seeing what I had done, I started to cry. Here was not my boxing opponent, here was my beloved brother with a bloody nose I had caused. Sensing my despair, Charlie tried to calm me down, no matter that blood was spurting from his nose. This commotion brought my sister downstairs, and I tried to explain to her, through my tears, "{Sob} I hit Charlie on the nose, Margie. I didn't {sob} mean to, but I did, and that's why he's bleeding. I'm so {sob} sorry, Char." I may have won that fight (as I won them all), but I didn't want to win it like that.

Oh, and the tackle football games Charlie and I played in the narrow entry hall of our house on those Saturday mornings. In one of those games, Charlie kicked off and the ball sailed right into the stained glass transom window above the front door, breaking one of its panels. My brother somehow never won any of those games either.

How I loved those Saturday morning events. I imagine everyone else in the family did, too, since it gave them a few extra hours of sleep upstairs on the second floor they would not have had otherwise. How I loved the living room that magically turned into a boxing ring, and the entry hallway that turned into a football gridiron, every Saturday morning. And how I loved (and still love) my brother, Charlie, or, as he was known then to his friends, Champ. He may have always pronounced me "the winner and still 'champeen,'" but he's always been my champ.

My knight in shining armor, Charlie literally rescued me from bodily harm one day. As I was playing by myself in the alley behind our house, an unfriendly neighborhood dog, a black-tongued Chow named Roxy, started to chase me. I ran like hell to avoid getting bitten and reached the narrow passageway alongside our garage leading from the alley into our back yard just as the dog was closing in on me. Charlie was practicing lacrosse in the yard, throwing a lacrosse ball against the back wall of the garage and catching it with his lacrosse stick, when he heard me screaming and scrambling to get into our yard. Seeing his little brother trying to outrun the dog, he pointed his lacrosse stick into the dog's snout and held it at bay to keep it from any further pursuit while I escaped into the back yard.

Another time Charlie championed our family was when he, Margie, and I were walking in Druid Hill Park a few blocks from our house. A bunch of boys his age from the much-feared Francis Street gang came down the hill and blocked our way. "Hey, Jews, where ya' goin'?" one of them asked in their usual threatening tone. Charlie interposed himself between his two siblings and the three Francis Streeters. Using mild words in a conversational voice, he attempted to talk them away from my sister and me, but the gang would have none of it. Soon fiercer words were exchanged, and one of the Francis Street toughs punched Charlie in the face. It wasn't a terribly hard blow, but immediately Charlie fell to the ground and started "sobbing." As his little brother, I could tell it was fake sobbing, but it was enough to make the Francis Streeters think they had prevailed, and so they sauntered off, satisfied that they had laid low another Jew-boy.

Then there was the time the three of us were walking in Druid Hill Park on the way to Carlin's Amusement Park during a presidential election season. Francis Streeters accosted us again, demanding of my brother "Who ya' votin' for?" Reflecting Mom's and Dad's staunch support of Roosevelt, Charlie replied, "Roosevelt," whereupon he was battered with punches. On the way home, the same toughs stopped us again and asked the same question. Smarter this time, Charlie replied "Dewey," but they pummeled him again anyway. With the Francis Streeters, sometimes even our smarts couldn't keep us out of harm's way.

Charlie and I were so close that he asked me, when I was 14, to serve as his best man for his wedding that June to Marilyn. I was proud as punch to have the honor, and at so tender an age, too. For the wedding, both Charlie and I were decked out in rented tuxedos with stiffly starched board-front shirts and collars. The Shaarei Tfiloh synagogue, where the wedding took place, was not air-conditioned, so, as the bride and groom stood at the dais, and the cantor and rabbi intoned the marriage cere-mony in Hebrew, I conscientiously performed my best man duties by wiping the sweat off Charlie's brow. I did not notice, until too late, that I, too, was suffering from the summer's heat and humidity inside the synagogue. Halfway into the ceremony, I started to see black dots before my eyes and began to feel faint. The cantor noticed me wavering and about to fall to the floor, and, interrupting the wedding ceremony and calling for Charlie's assistance, he and Charlie helped me to a nearby chair. I've carried the memory of that embarrassing incident with me the rest of my life. If Charlie ever questioned his choice of best man, he's made no mention of it to me, and it had no impact on our relationship.

Although I was their beloved little brother—"the baby of the family," my mother called me, much to my chagrin—my other brothers and sister were not quite as close to me as Charlie was, mainly because of their greater distance in age from me. Not that the family didn't do things together while we were all living at home, such as outings to nearby Druid Hill Park for a picnic or to the zoo there, or to the boat lake in the park to rent a rowboat, or three miles further out to the city's western edge to picnic in Leakin Park. Sometimes two or three of the children of the family would go downtown to the Hippodrome Theater to see a movie followed by a live stage show. The Spike Jones Band, whose musical tomfoolery delighted its audiences, was one of our favorite Hippodrome live shows. Around Christmas time, Mom, Dad, and whichever of the kids wanted to would go downtown to see the fantastic Christmas window displays—

with moving Santas and jolly elves, sleighs loaded with gift-wrapped presents, electric trains circling around—that the major department stores always mounted.

Until I was 10 years old, Margie was unmarried and still living at home. She was the one who had most charge of me whenever Mom left the house for whatever reasons. If the baby-sitting was at night, I often ended up in Margie's bedroom at the back of the house due to the "high-highs." Because the bedroom I shared with Charlie was in the front of the house, whenever cars passed down the street at night, their headlights shone through the window blinds, making eerie, moving light patterns on the bedroom ceiling and wall. I was deathly afraid of these "high-highs," as I inexplicably named them, if I was in my bed alone, and the only thing that would calm me down was moving to Margie's room facing the back yard, where there were no "high-highs," until Mom came home.

Margie married when she was 18, whereupon she left Goucher College after her first year there and moved to Brook-lyn with her new husband, Lenny. They met at a U.S.O. dance when Lenny was in the Army. Margie had begged my mother to let her drive the family car to the dance with some girlfriends. Mom was reluctant to let her drive at night but agreed to let her go only if Margie promised to telephone home the moment she arrived at the dance. When she arrived and went to the phone booth in the U.S.O. hall, a soldier was in it talking away. After patiently waiting a few minutes, Margie gestured to the soldier that she had to make a call. The soldier smiled a broad smile, winked at my sister, and continued gabbing, telling jokes and laughing, all the while glancing slyly at the poor girl waiting to use the phone. After several more tries, and several more rebuffs from the Army in the person of this awful soldier, Margie—now almost in tears—interrupted his conversation and told him it was of the utmost importance that she use the phone to call her mother. The soldier, whose name was Lenny, gave up the phone booth and asked her to dance after she finished her call.

A prince of a fellow, Lenny regaled the family with jokes and magic tricks when he came to court my sister. He was very proficient in performing these tricks. I was fascinated and yet puzzled by them, and both Margie and the rest of the family were beguiled by Lenny. Once he popped the question, I wanted to buy them my own gift for their wedding. After all, my beloved (and only) sister was getting married to a great guy, so I thought I would get them a wedding present worthy of the occasion. I took myself to Goffman's Hobby Shop in downtown Baltimore to shop for one—it was safe in those days for a nine-year-old to venture downtown on a streetcar by himself. Once there, I looked at Goffman's collection of little figurines I had noticed during an earlier visit to the store. Upon selecting a brightly glazed miniature ceramic animal and paying the munificent sum of $1.10 for it, I took my prize home and wrapped it up as my wedding gift for Margie and Lenny.

After they were married, I visited them a couple of times in the Bensonhurst section of Brooklyn where they lived. When I was older and Margie and Lenny were then living outside of Washington in the 1950s, I went to live with them during the summer I worked at the National Institutes of Health.

During night baby-sitting episodes, Bill was the one to take charge of seeing that I ate whatever dinner Mom left for the family. Picky eater that I was, it was not easy duty for him. He persisted more than the others in trying to get me to eat what Mom had laid out.

Bill was the only one of my brothers to serve in the military. He was drafted into the Army at the height of the Korean War, which caused everyone else in the family great consternation. Fortunately, he did not have to serve overseas: The army thought his engineering skills were best put to use stateside. I remember visiting him when he was stationed at nearby Fort Belvoir, Virginia, and being so proud of him in his crisp khaki uniform. When I was 14, he married Sunnie and moved away from home to establish their own household.

My oldest brother, Leonard, contracted polio as a young child during one of the country's periodic epidemics. Part of the treatment required him to be in strict isolation in the hospital—no visitors at all. My parents told of how they "visited" him at the hospital by standing outside the building, looking up at the window of the room he was in, and, with tears in their eyes, waving to let him know they were there and concerned about him. After he was released from the hospital, he had to undergo a heavy exercise regimen of forced movement of his limbs, which my mother conscientiously carried out in order to preserve what could be preserved of his muscle strength.

My maternal grandmother directed her unmarried youngest daughter, Rhona, to live with our family for about a year to help my mother out during this crisis. Aunt Rhona recalls aiding in Leonard's recovery by regularly rubbing cocoa butter on his legs. She also recalls that, for the rest of her life, the odor of cocoa butter wreaked havoc with her stomach. Another of Mom's sisters, Mildred, a nurse, spelled Mom whenever she could to give her a break in the exhausting, physically challenging regimen that it was my mother's responsibility to perform, day in and day out, for over a year. While Leonard did recover much of his limb movement, he was left with a permanently atrophied bicep and diminished strength in his left arm. Later, he also was blinded in one eye at the age of nine when a playmate shot him in the eye using a homemade bow and arrow.

Len courted his wife, Elinor, in an old, green Chevrolet coupe he had bought. They sometimes invited me to accompany them on their dates. On those occasions, I would wedge myself onto the ledge behind the front—and only—seat of the coupe, where Len and Elinor sat, as we drove to whatever destination they had in mind. Around that time I had learned the concept of being "a burden" to another person, and I always asked Len and El if I would be "a burden to them" if they took me along on their dates. They always assured me I would not be.

On one of their dates, they went out into the country to rent horses to ride. They plopped me on a horse, too. I had been on horses a few times before that, but in different circumstances and on different kinds of horses. There used to be men who would bring around a tired, docile pony to the city streets and take, and then sell, photos of the neighborhood young ones sitting on the pony—sometimes appearing none too happy to be doing so. It gave city kids a feel for what the country was like and left their families with photographic proof, as well. And there was also a small horse ring at Carlin's Park, one of the city amusement parks we would sometimes go to, that offered rides on ponies. There, your parent or sibling paid money and a handler would plop you on a pony and lead it around in a circle a few times. But those were ponies and, now, on this date with Len and El, I was placed on a full-grown horse, far off the ground and with no handler to keep me secure. As I looked down at how far I was off the ground on this huge beast, with no one around to handle it, it scared the living daylights out of me. I adamantly refused to ride it. Although they didn't mention it afterward, I think I was a burden to Leonard and Elinor on that date.

Fourteen years older than me, Leonard married and left home when I was 11. He and Elinor asked me to be the "official" photographer at their wedding at the Beth Jacob synagogue, which they kept low-key in order to keep the expenses down. I proudly assented, using my Kodak camera with black-and-white film to record the event, the blue-tinted flashbulbs popping away throughout the ceremony and the reception afterward.

A few short years after getting married and leaving home, Leonard, by then a lawyer, ran for a City Council seat in Baltimore's 4th District. In doing so, he challenged the candidate backed by the James H. "Jack" Pollack political machine for that seat. Gilbert Sandler, in his book *Jewish Baltimore: A Family Album*, describes the Pollack machine thus: "Northwest Baltimore was linked to the patronage system, and Jack Pollack

controlled it. . . . Largess to loyalists was the game; in Northwest
Baltimore Jack Pollack was master of that game." Len recruited
me, barely in my teens, to help him in his campaign. I went
door-to-door leafleting homes in our neighborhood. On some
nights, I accompanied him in his old, green Chevy coupe, which
he had outfitted with a loudspeaker on the roof, as he drove
through the various neighborhoods of the 4th District and
announced campaign messages into the microphone. I also
made some of the announcements myself in order to give
Leonard a chance to rest his voice. Len lost the election, but he
garnered the largest vote count up to that time for any 4th District
City Council candidate opposing a Pollack-backed candidate.

Before he died in 2013 at the age of 88, Leonard went on
to fight other uphill battles, including successfully arguing the
landmark *Murray v. Curlett* case before the U.S. Supreme
Court in 1963 that, consolidated with the *Abington School District v. Schempp* case, resulted in ending mandatory prayer
recitation in U.S. public schools. Leonard's victory in that
church-state separation case for his client, Madalyn Murray,
occasioned a flood of hate mail to him. He framed and posted
on his law office wall a few of the more colorful letters he
received. The most vituperative one ended with this stirring
message: "I hope you rot in hell, you dirty, rotten, Communist,
Jew bastard."

Besides Charlie, Margie, Billy, and Leonard, our family
also had "adopted" members. The alleys behind the houses in
the neighborhood supported a large number of alley cats. Regularly, our family would "adopt" one of the cats as
"ours"—usually one that was brave enough to come into our
back yard and lurk on the small wooden landing near our back
door. We didn't really own them, and we did not let them into
the house. But we fed, petted, and played with them, and so
they became our de facto family pets. I named each according
to their appearance: "Spot," black with a white spot on his
throat;"Tiger," light gray with dark gray stripes; "Calico," who

was, well, a calico cat; and my favorite of all "Nocturne," an all-black cat with only the lightest touches of white on the tips of her ears. She was slight, sleek, and smooth and reminded me of a panther. I loved the way she slithered sinuously around my ankles to rub up against me, just begging me to pet her. After many months of coming around to our back door where we left food for her and played with her, Nocturne stopped showing up one day. Why would she do that? I asked my family. I suspect they knew why, but they did not let on to me their fears of what might have befallen Nocturne. A short time later, I saw an all-black cat lying dead at the end of the alley that ran behind our house, evidently having been run over by a car. It was Nocturne, I was sure of it. I ran home, crying, as fast as I could and told everyone in the family what had happened. They tried to console me, but for hours I just sat on the stairs leading off our hallway crying over Nocturne's fate.

Our house being so close to Druid Hill Park, at night I could hear the lions in the park's zoo roar. It was eerie to hear that sound in the middle of the city in the dead of night. Being so close to the park, too, the whole family would go often into the park on weekends to visit the zoo. In the summer, the lawn in front of the zoo's Mansion House was the site of open-air concerts by a municipal band. We brought chairs and blankets and there partook of the free concerts while obtaining some relief from the heat. A highlight of those concerts was the sing-along, where the words of popular tunes were projected onto a large screen at the side of the bandstand. The audience would "follow the bouncing ball" as it hopped to each word of the song's lyrics and sing along. Another attraction in the park was the boat lake. I went there often with one or another of my siblings where, for a modest amount, we rented gray wooden rowboats in the summer to flit about in the decent-sized artificial lake. And when winter came, we could go to the boat lake to skate—for free.

It was there in the winter when Charlie was speeding on his racing skates that he tripped and slid about 10 yards on his stomach, smacking his head against the island in the middle of the lake. Fortunately, our Uncle Leonard, a physician, was living on Holmes Avenue at the time, so Char was taken to Uncle Len's house to have his wound stitched up. He still bears the scar under his left eyebrow as a reminder of that accident.

Like many families, we amused ourselves by gathering around the radio in our den to listen to the programs that aired at night. Comedies: The Jack Benny Show, Fred Allen, Fibber McGee and Molly, Amos 'n' Andy, Burns and Allen, Lum and Abner, the Aldrich Family. Dramas: Grand Central Station, Lux Radio Theater. Quiz shows: Information Please, Quiz Kids, The $64 Question (a lot of money in those days!), It Pays to Be

Ignorant (a quiz show spoof—and, yes, that was its actual title). Music: The Hit Parade and the bands of Kay Kyser, Artie Shaw, Tommy Dorsey, and Les Brown and his Band of Renown. And with all the lights turned out, the mystery programs: The Shadow ("Who knows what evil lurks in the minds of men? The Shadow knows."), Suspense ("Tales well-calculated to keep you in [dramatic organ chords] . . . suspense"), The Inner Sanctum [Cr-e-e-a-a-k].

Sometimes I went with my father to his furniture upholstering establishment to "work" alongside him and my grandfather. It was in a cavernous old brick building with wooden floors on 21 North High Street, a building that, coincidentally, housed in the late 1800s, in a rented room, the Baltimore Talmud Torah (Hebrew school). Dad's business was located near the Shot Tower, a still-standing Baltimore landmark harkening back to the Civil War era, where musket balls were made by dropping hot lead from the top of the brick tower to be cooled in a pool of water at the bottom many feet below. Dad always called his place near the Shot Tower "the factory," and I guess it was, as it took wooden furniture frames he had bought and then added springs, padding, and upholstery to transform them into finished furniture pieces. It wasn't a factory in the sense that large machines churned out finished products; rather, the work was done by hand, one piece of furniture at a time.

Dad's father worked there with him, his main job being to cut upholstery fabric, at which he was quite skilled. This was an important job, for a bad cut would ruin many dollars worth of material. I liked to watch Grandpa David place a cardboard pattern cutout on top of several layers of fabric and then snip along its edges to produce the needed pieces of material. I often found ways to play with the leftover scraps of fabric after he finished cutting it, making fanciful make-believe animals with them. Grandpa was a skilled craftsman in other areas as well: He made a wooden dollhouse for my sister Margie, complete with miniature furniture and electric lights.

Once Grandpa David cut the fabric, other workers padded the frames, covered them with the chosen fabrics, and, with mouths full of furniture tacks, affixed the fabric to the frames, spitting the tacks out one at a time onto the magnetic end of their upholstery hammers and then banging them into the covered furniture frame. At a time when household items were less disposable than they are now, people had their furniture recovered once the original fabric had worn out, rather than discard it, so a large part of Dad's business was reupholstering furniture as well. The place at 21 North High Street always had a definite wood smell that I liked, not surprising since it contained wooden furniture frames and wood shavings.

On some evenings in the summer, when Dad got home from work on the rare occasions that it was not too late, before he would even eat the supper Mom had waiting for him, he would take us kids to Moe's, a neighborhood variety store, for snowballs. These five-cent treats of crushed ice topped with the syrup of our choice—my favorite was chocolate—were served up in disposable, flat-bottomed drinking cups. They were not quite the same as today's sno-cones or Hawaiian shave ice; they had a distinctly different mouth-feel to them. The thin, flat wooden spoon provided with them was used to shovel the flavored crushed ice into our mouths. I can still recall the gritty feel of the ice in my mouth and the sweet flavor of the syrup as I crunched into the snowballs.

On weekends, if my father could spare going into work on a Sunday, we all piled into "the machine" for a drive to various places in the country—the country being any place on the outskirts of Baltimore. After all, gasoline cost only 13 cents a gallon, so our outings were an affordable form of entertainment. One of my favorite places to visit, which I suspect was Dad's, too, was Curtiss-Wright Air Field at the then-sparsely populated very northwest corner of the city. There we would stand outside the fence and watch the planes take off and land. Although my own first flight in a plane did not occur until I turned 20, I was fascinated with flying from an early age and remain so to this day.

Sometimes the family visited Willy Mayer, the foreman in my father's furniture factory, and his family. Especially at Christmas-time, a visit to Willy's Baltimore row house was an exciting event. Every Christmas, Willy moved all the furniture out of his dining room and living room to set up platforms for his holiday display, a display for which he achieved local fame for its expanse and authenticity. It encompassed an extensive toy electric train setup, with several types of trains traveling on a complex system of rails through miniature tunnels, forests, and towns, choo-chooing along and occasionally tooting their whistles. Along the train routes, laid out on the platforms, miniature railroad crossing guards came out to swing a lantern as they lowered the crossing gate, tiny cars came along and then stopped at the crossing, and miniature children came out of their schoolhouse to see the trains pass. Farther along into "the country," the little electric trains went through hills where tiny skiers went up on a chair lift and then skiied down, skaters circled a pond, and a miniature horse and sleigh pranced in the snow. As a six-, seven-, and eight-year-old, I was delighted and fascinated by Willy's Christmas garden. So many electric trains, such realistic tiny skiers and skaters.

Willy also had a house on one of the tributaries that laced the landscape near Annapolis, Maryland. He sometimes invited our family to visit him there, and it was there that I had my first experience fishing. With my father watching, Willy taught me how to bait the hook, fix the bob, and cast the line into the water (after a fashion). I caught a small sunfish on my first fishing outing there and for weeks afterward enthusiastically showed the photo of me holding it to friends and relatives. I worried, though, about whether or not the fish felt the pain of the hook in its mouth, and for a long time afterward, I was filled with guilt for my part in the sunfish's demise.

Occasionally, our family went farther afield on day excursions to take a two-hour boat ride to a local resort area called Tolchester on the other side of the Chesapeake Bay. In my adulthood, my memory of that place and that name has become so distant that I almost feel that I might have imagined it. It exists as a dreamy place in my mind, enveloped in mists. Saying the word "Tolchester" now conjures up a fuzzy mental picture of an old-fashioned carousel twirling, twirling in swirling mists, music from a calliope playing an amusement park tune as the wooden horses and the little boys and the little girls go twirling, twirling, around and around.

I know it was real, for I had been there with my family, probably three or four times in the 1940s, but so long ago that sometimes now it seems more fantastical than real to me. My parents told me the first time I was to go with the family to Tolchester that, to get there, you had to go on the ocean—really the Chesapeake Bay. The ocean: "What was that?" I asked. "It's like a big lake," they told me, "so big you can't see the other end of it." *How could a lake be that big?* I asked myself, my only point of reference at the time being the boat lake in Druid Hill Park. The answer to that question dumfounded five-year-old me; I couldn't envision a lake so large that I couldn't see its other side.

Although Baltimore was on an outlet to the Chesapeake Bay, I had no experience of the water at that time, be it bay, inlet, or ocean. We lived eight miles from Baltimore harbor, but it might as well have been eight countries away for all I had seen of it up to that point. The boat lake in the park was it for my experience of bodies of water, much less really big bodies of water. When my parents first said we were going to Tolchester on a "big, high boat," I was frightened about how we would get from the land onto the boat, and, once we had made it onto the boat, frightened about what would keep us from falling off it into the water. Until I first saw the gangplank in Baltimore Harbor, there so high in the sky, connecting the boat to the land, I simply could not imagine how humans made the transition from land to boat. I wasn't happy walking up the gangplank my first time to step onto the boat bound for Tolchester.

The Old Line, a blog about Maryland past and present, has this to say about Tolchester's history:

> In its prime in the 1950s and early 1960s, Tolchester Beach expanded to 155 acres and was serviced by six steamers and a ferry. There were to be found a dance hall, a roller coaster, bowling alleys, a bingo parlor, a roller skating rink, the whip, dodgems, pony and goat carts, boat rides, a miniature steam train named Jumbo, novelty and candy shops, and popcorn, ice cream, hot dogs and kewpie doll stands. At its height, Tolchester Beach attracted as many as 20,000 visitors a weekend from across the bay and the Eastern Shore of Maryland, but after flourishing for 85 years, Tolchester Beach passed from the scene, finally closing in 1962.

Now when I think of Tolchester, I still envision a dreamy place, with an old-fashioned carousel twirling, twirling in swirling mists, music from a calliope playing an amusement park tune as the horses and the little boys and the little girls go twirling, twirling, around and around.

3

FROM WHENCE THEY CAME

"In the innocent childhood of [the 20th] century the Russian-
Jewish Pale of Settlement was the disgrace of Western
humanity, the last word in reaction and brutality."

— Maurice Samuel, *The World of Sholom Aleichem*

FROM THE LATE 18th century into the early 20th century,
Jews in Russia were required to live in the Pale of Settlement, where both Khodorkov and Dvinsk are to be found. The
Pale was an area in the western part of the Russian empire
stretching from the Baltic Sea on the north to the Black Sea on
the south. In that area, Jews were allowed to live—indeed *had*
to live unless they practiced certain professions that enabled
them to live "beyond the Pale" to serve the majority population
outside the Pale of Settlement. Living in the *shtetlach* of the
Pale, Jews were denied education past a certain level, entrance
into certain professions, and economic advancement past a
certain ceiling. And they were persecuted physically through
depredations and pogroms carried out by Cossacks and others.
They were forced to be, and so were, a people apart. As Jewish
historian and critic Maurice Samuel wrote in *The World of
Sholom Aleichem*, "It was a principal of Russian law that every-

thing was forbidden to Jews unless specifically permitted. . . . Within the vast semi-ghetto which was the Pale and outside of which the Jews could not settle, Jewish life grew and unfolded. . . . [The Jews] managed to survive and even flourish. But their prosperity was spiritual rather than material."

My parents and grandparents left their mother country, with hopes high, for a better life in the United States. It was a life they anticipated would hold greater educational opportunities for their children than were available to them in Russia, opportunities they most sorely lacked in the old country. Although the poverty, persecution, and pogroms of the old country motivated them to leave, it still must have taken an inordinate amount of courage on the part of my grandparents to leave their parents (my great-grandparents) behind—never to see them again—to come to a country where they did not know the language, were uncertain how they would eke out a living, and had few other relatives there. My parents, especially my father—who remembered the old country more vividly than my mother did—so loved and appreciated this golden land, the United States, that they would never tolerate anyone casting aspersions on it. Here was a place, they believed, where they and their children could be educated to whatever level their talents allowed, earn their living however they wished, and feel that they and their families could be, if not an integral part of the larger society, at least safe within that society.

My parents worked hard (as did their children) and achieved a modicum of comfort and pride in their accomplishments in the United States. But even though my father appreciated the opportunities his adopted country gave him, he did not disown completely the country of his birth. He retained some knowledge of Russian into adulthood and kept his Russian birth certificate all his life. It was not an actual birth certificate issued by the government, however. It was a document headed "This is from the book of birth of Jews who were born in the village of Khodorkov, Skvirsky County in the year 1900" and signed by the Skvirsky County rabbi. I suppose this was the authorities' way to document the birth of a Jew while enforcing the Jews' separateness from the rest of the population.

Dad remembers living as a boy in a two-story house about two miles from the center of Khodorkov. Its four bedrooms accommodated the family of ten where, he recalled in a brightly written account of his childhood, "we were comfortable and happy." A barn outside housed the family's two cows, and a large garden grew all the vegetables the family needed. Often during the long winters—with frigid temperatures and snow covering the ground from October through March—he and his playmates would tie home-made ice skates to their shoes and skate on the town pond. In the heat of summer, he remembered, the children played outdoors, their bare feet stirring up dust clouds as they engaged in hide-and-go-seek or kite-flying on the sun-baked soil.

In a letter he wrote to me after I had moved away from home, my father provided a description of the town of his birth. It is amazing how vivid his memories were, given that he left Russia when he was just 11 years old:

> We lived outside the town on the . . . main country road that ran from the town to the next village. Across the road was the town hospital. Farther up toward the town was the Catholic church and Levandowsky's estate. Levandowsky was a Polish large landowner who must have owned half the town, then as you continued toward the town you came to the colossal sugar refinery owned by Halperin, a Jew (believe it or not). There were, you heard of here and there, some wealthy Jews. Farther down and on the right was the sand quarry where they mined sand and gravel. Then you reached the town. There was the very large Orthodox Russian cathedral where in the compound lived the Orthodox priest and his family (they marry) and where your Aunt Manya . . . found literary friends among the priest's several daughters. She used to borrow books from them and often carried home an armful. The priest, as I recollect, was a very learned and liberal man who respected (as my impression goes) other religions and who did not even try to convert your Aunt Manya. . . . To continue on with my travelogue, the town as I guess must have had a population of about 25,000 consisting of Russians, Poles, and Jews. Remember, the Ukraine was once dominated by Poland. There were stores, shops, some ghettos, and even a cobblestone main street with street lamps, but alas no public school,

and that was one reason your Grandpa and Grandma brought us to America where there are no cobblestone paved streets (only gold paving is used), but with plenty of schools.

And so, that is the reason my son, you are a native American. . . .

———— · · ————

In Khodorkov, my father's father, David Kerpelman, was a foreman in Halperin's sugar beet refinery. David was the son of Yail and Dvorah Kerpelman; he married Clara, the daughter of Yail's brother Yontil and his wife Sara. In other words, David and Clara, my paternal grandparents, were cousins. This was not unusual among Jews of the *shtetlach*, where the number of eligible partners of like religion was limited. There were about 3,700 Jews living in Khodorkov at the end of the 19th century when they got married. Clara came from a nearby *shtetl* in Ukraine.

David was a slight, mild-mannered man. Clara was almost the same height as her husband and had a few pounds on him. Together, David and Clara raised their brood of eight living children, of whom my father was their fifth. Two other children had died at a very young age. When they decided to leave Khodorkov, the family traveled to Germany, there to take a ship to the United States and their new life. In March 1912, my grandmother, grandfather, and seven of their eight children (one of whom was my father) boarded the S.S. Frankfurt in Bremerhaven bound for the United States. The ship was a recently built one. The fact that it held no first class passengers, only 108 second class passengers, but 1,889 third class (steerage) passengers suggests it was built specifically to take advantage of the early 20th century migration wave.

Once as an adult, during a business trip to Washington, D.C., I visited the National Archives and obtained a copy of the ship's manifest for the voyage to the U.S. of my father's family. In it is an enumeration of pertinent details of all the ship's passengers on that voyage. There, David, my grandfather, is listed as age 46, five feet eight inches tall, with blond hair and gray eyes, and in good health. Clara, my grandmother, is described as age 36, five feet eight inches in height, and with gray hair and gray eyes. The seven children accompanying them are also duly described, among them "Moses" (my father, Morris), age 11. The family is further listed as being of the Hebrew race and having $111 with them—about $2,700 in today's dollars—with which to start a new life in the new world. On March 21, 1912, the S.S. Frankfurt docked in Philadelphia, from where my paternal grandparents and their children traveled to Baltimore to live with an uncle, Hyman Koppelman, for two weeks until they could gain a footing in the New World.

While on its return transatlantic voyage eastbound from Galveston, Texas to Bremerhaven a few short weeks later, the S.S. Frankfurt was among the seven vessels documented to have received the S.O.S. signal the R.M.S. Titanic, 153 miles away, sent out as it was sinking.

The eighth child in the family, the oldest daughter, Manya, stayed behind when her parents and siblings left Khodorkov, as she was already married. She and her husband emigrated to the United States after World War I, settling in Chicago. Aunt Manya's tale of escape from Russia with her husband in the 1920s is a harrowing one. They took with them as much of

their family "riches" as they could in the form of gold that Manya secreted within the seams of her petticoats and skirts. At each checkpoint and border crossing on their land journey to their ship, she had to put up with the border guards feeling up

LIST OR MANIFEST OF ALIEN

Required by the regulations of the Secretary of Commerce and Labor of the United States, under

S.S. _____ sailing from _____

her skirts, as much for their sensual pleasure as for their duty to ensure she had nothing of value hidden on her. She managed to get to the United States with both her virtue and her family's gold intact.

My grandfather David worked as a fabric cutter in my father's upholstered furniture business for as many years as his health allowed. He frequently conducted many of the traditional *seders* (Passover dinners), at our house, insisting on reading the *haggadah* (the ceremonial text), all the way through in Hebrew to the very end without skipping a word. This caused the annual *seders* to last for hours, despite protestations from the children of our family to "Skip a couple of pages, Grandpa" and "Hurry it along." How I envied other families who did skip parts of the ceremony. I had, however, my own way of checking out of the seemingly interminable ritual. David and Clara made their own wine from a Concord grape vine that climbed up a trellis to their back porch, and the heavy, extremely sweet, red wine they prepared and served during the *seders* usually put me to sleep long before the *seder* itself was over.

As the youngest around the table, it traditionally fell to me to ask, in Hebrew, the four questions that kicked off the *seder* narrative, a retelling of the story of the Jews' exodus from Egypt. I always undertook my part in this ritual with some pride, but also with some trepidation lest my pronunciation in Hebrew elicit a correction from my grandfather.

Of my four grandparents, I was probably least close to *Bubbe* (grandmother) Clara, not for any particular reason but just that she was a reticent woman, and she was the least familiar with the English language of my four grandparents. But she always plied me with *kikhlach* (cookies) when I visited. She also made pickled tomatoes for my father, for which I soon also acquired a taste.

In their later years, my paternal grandparents, David and Clara Kerpelman, lived in a small row house on Boarman Avenue just off Reisterstown Road in northwest Baltimore. One day, when I was 14, I walked over to their house by myself to pay them a visit. Clara was on her front stoop and saw me approaching. She must have thought I was another young neighborhood punk out to harass them, and she shooed me away. A sensitive kid to begin with, I felt terribly sad at this rebuff; I left with the empty feeling that my own grandmother did not even know me. When I told my father what had occurred, he went to great lengths to assure me that his aged mother's vision was so poor she likely didn't recognize me. I felt a little better after that, but, unfortunately, the memory of that incident is the most vivid one I have of her.

Not long ago, my brother Charlie told me a touching story of his own. As an adult, Charlie's work in Switzerland as a consultant in disaster management for the United Nations took him on frequent missions to foreign countries. He was on a consultancy mission to Tbilisi in the former Soviet republic of Georgia where, as usual, he arranged to stay with a local family rather than at a hotel in order to get to know the locale and the people better. When the matron of the family first opened the door to him, he was briefly speechless as a familiar odor wafted into his nostrils—the precise old country odor of our grandparents' homes. If that weren't enough of a pleasant shock, on the balcony of that house in Tbilisi, Georgia was a trellis covered over with grape vines, just like at our grandparents' house on Boarman Avenue in Baltimore, Maryland, U.S.A., almost six thousand miles and many years distant.

As for my maternal grandparents, my mother's father, Ellis Kurland, was a butcher from Dvinsk who served in the quartermaster corps of the Tsar's army. My mother's mother, Sarah Schain, was born in 1880 in a small town in Poland, but with border changes the town is now in the Grodno district of Byelorussia (now called Belarus). The town's name had been variously rendered in English as Svislotch, Svisloc, Sislovitch, Sislevitch, Svislovits, Svisloch, and Swislocz. Sarah was born in the "Poor Jewish Neighbourhood," as it was delineated on one map, in the southeast corner of the town.

In 1880, when Sarah was but a few days old, her mother, Chasha, age 33, died, leaving her and her siblings "orphans"— a term commonly applied in her time to children after their mother died, even if the father were still alive, as was the case with Sarah's. In a handwritten account of her childhood, written in the broken, rudimentary English Sarah learned once she was in the U.S., she recounts rather dreamily how her childhood then progressed: "Then begin awful sadness, quiet nights dark days for the young unlucky orphans. [At the age of eight, Sarah] went to a dressmaker to learn a trade. For three long years, without wages during the three year [working] from seven in the morning until nine in the night. Surely it was necessary."

Her father, Moshe David Schain, remarried a short time after his first wife's death, and he went on to have another five children with his second wife, Esther. It is apparent that Sarah did not like her stepmother. Continuing her story in the third person, Sarah writes autobiographically:

> She thought I am old enough, and it is for me necessary to leave my home my born house my born city, and going far far away in the big world. . . . [S]he did not like to live in an atmosphere where you did not have your best friend [her birth mother]. Her childhood heart was dreaming for something better. It was a summer day when children in her age was playing, but she thought, I am big enough to know the big world. Then was she saying to her father, I would like to go in the city, Bialystok, which her father's father was living there.

Although her father tried to talk her out of it, Sarah's mind was made up and, at the tender age of 12, she moved to the larger city of Bialystok, 25 miles away, to live with either her grandfather or an uncle (the family record is unclear) and to be apprenticed to a seamstress. There, Sarah labored away into her teen years sewing articles of clothing.

It is told within my family that the man who would later become my maternal grandfather, Ellis Kurland, was strutting down a street in Bialystock one day on army business, proudly wearing his finest military uniform. He noticed through a window a seamstress, her head down, intent on her sewing. After seeing this *schaine madel* (beautiful girl) sewing in the same window for several days running, he bought shirting material one day and brought it to the shop to have several shirts made by this beautiful girl. He told her, "I want these shirts made, but you don't have to hurry. I'll come in . . . when they're ready." For several weeks running he stopped in regularly "to see how they were coming along."

Ellis ardently pursued this girl, often courting her in his military finery. Finally, after six months of this, on a day when Sarah's step-mother was visiting, he rode up to where she was staying on—as Sarah's niece described it many years later—"a horse, a beautiful red horse—I'll never forget that horse . . . and a handsome man with a lot of brass buttons and a lot of trimming was riding on [the] horse. And he came riding right to our place . . . and walked in." He asked for Sarah's hand in marriage and, after several more weeks of cajoling and persuading, her family agreed to let her marry this gruff, rough, tough army man. In 1899, at the age of 19, Sarah married Ellis Kurland and moved away with him to Dvinsk.

In 1904, Ellis crossed the Atlantic from Liverpool, England, bound for New York on the S.S. Baltic to establish himself in the U.S. A year later, now in Baltimore, he sent for Sarah and their three young children at the time—my mother's older sister, Helen (whose given name was Ida), my mother, Fannie, and their younger brother, Milton. The other seven siblings in Mom's family were born in the United States. The entire family became naturalized United States citizens in 1914.

Sarah's older brother, Jona, emigrated to Sweden in the early 1900s, to survive and live to an old age. By leaving Dvinsk early in the 20th century, Sarah and Jona and their children avoided the Holocaust that was to be visited upon the Jews four decades later. But Sarah left behind her three full-sisters in the city of their birth, Svislotch. I never knew these great-aunts: Chai Faiga, Dvorah, and Fruma Leah. In 1942 the Germans— as they did in so many other towns in that region—gathered all the Jews in Svislotch (some 3,500 of them) and loaded the able-bodied into carts to be taken to work camps, concentration camps, or the Volkovisk Ghetto. The rest—mostly children and older women—were led to a nearby forest and murdered. By the war's end, only 42 of the Jews of Svislotch had survived. It is believed that Grandma Sarah's three sisters were among the Jews whom the Germans marched into the Wyszbinik Forest and shot. I write "believed" because Grandma Sarah was ever reluctant to talk about the old country.

And so it was also for Dvinsk, the city Sarah and Ellis left after they were married in order to come to America. In 1913, there were 32,400 Jews in Dvinsk, comprising 43% of that city's population. Various aggressions in the years that followed caused the Jewish population to decrease to 13,000. During World War II, as the Germans occupied the city, non-Jewish Latvians eagerly organized what the Germans called "self-purging actions," in which the local Latvians systematically murdered the city's Jewish population. One writer, Leni Yahil, characterized the Latvians as "among the more savage collab-orators with the Nazis." Only 1,000 Jews remained alive in Dvinsk by the end of that war.

All four of my grandparents were very much "old country," and the sights and smells in their homes evoked a land very distant. Their houses always were redolent of a slightly stale, old country odor, which presented to my nose as a mixture of boiled chicken and boiled onion. All four of my grandparents spoke only Yiddish, except Sarah, who, with great perseverance, learned a smattering of English. As a child, speaking with them was a difficult matter for me, as English was the only language in which I was then fluent. With the rudimentary Yiddish I gradually acquired listening to my parents and grandparents speak among themselves, and with my parents often serving as interpreters, I eventually managed some basic communication with my grandparents. But given the great distance in culture, language, and age between them and me, I never felt very close to them.

While I was growing up in Baltimore, my parents visited their parents at least once a week, and my brothers and sister and I went along with them on most of those visits. The weekly visit to my father's parents was almost a necessity, for whenever we visited them, my father would have to replenish the ice in their icebox because they did not have an electric refrigerator. To do that, he would go up the street to the other side of Reisterstown Road, often with me accompanying him, to the ice house, where he would put a quarter into a slot and then wait for a block of ice to slide down the chute to our waiting hands. We then wrapped it in burlap and wrestled it back to grandma and grandpa's house to place it in their icebox. This is probably the reason that my family always referred to our own refrigerator—even though it was an electric one by the time I was born—as an icebox.

Bubbe Sarah and *Zadie* Ellis, my mother's parents, lived in a Baltimore row house over Ellis's shop at 1925 West North Avenue, at the corner of Appleton Street, from where he butchered and sold kosher meat and poultry. Their kitchen had a window in it that looked into the butcher shop below, so if customers came in, Ellis or Sarah could go down the stairs to serve them. Sarah chose to work in the butcher shop so that her children would not have to. She was determined that every one of them obtain an education, and, with one exception, every one of them did earn a college degree.

My grandparents' prized possession, a metal samovar they

managed to take with them from Russia, held center place on
their dining room table. Whenever Ellis would drink *a glassele
tay* (a glass of tea), he did it old-country style, sipping the tea
through a hard rock of crystallized sugar held between his teeth
to sweeten the liquid as it went down.

Bubbe Sarah was a slight
woman who had silver-gray hair
for as long as I remember and,
in her later years, hands gnarled
by severe arthritis. She always
greeted   her   grandchildren
warmly with what we dubbed
"Grandma kisses"—heavy, wet
kisses on our cheeks. The aroma
of the *kikhlach* that she made
often permeated their house on
these visits, and *Bubbe* always
insisted that we take some whenever we visited. *Zadie* Ellis,
though of medium height, was a barrel-chested, sturdily-built
man who sported a gray goatee. He was a tough, direct person
whose mien communicated "Don't mess with me."   His
youngest daughter, my Aunt Rhona, recalls, "For as long as I
can remember, he never spoke . . . he always hollered."
Grandma's niece, Sarah Kaplan Kurland put it equally color-
fully: "You know, they say he used to holler. Alright, he
hollered—nobody's perfect."

That same niece also delightedly recalled in her later years
that when the ship in which she came to America a few years
after Grandma Sarah's did approached New York harbor, fire-
works lit up the sky (on what was probably the Fourth of July).
"I never vas so happy in mein whole life—coming to America
on George Vashington's boithday. All of us [passengers] fell on
the ground and kissed the floor. 'We are free! We are free! We
have no pogroms! We are free! Free people! Long live America!'

And we cried, and we danced . . . and we kissed each other . . . . . I'll never forget it."

Being a butcher, Ellis was so practiced in assessing the weight of meat in his butcher shop that he could lift me or one of my siblings up in the air when we were babies and estimate our weight to within a pound of our actual weight. He was so strong that, even into old age, he would delight in offering to shake each of his grandchildren's hands when we visited and then, with a sly grin on his face, squeeze our hands to the point of pain.

During World War II, *Zadie* Ellis sold meat on the black market. If a customer had the money to pay his prices, the customer could get meat from him "off" the ration cards that families were required to use during the war. He also made it a practice to surreptitiously rest his thumb on the scale whenever

he weighed out meat for his customers. *Bubbe* Sarah, kind soul that she was, would partially undo her husband's bad deeds by adding, while Ellis wasn't looking, a little extra on to the orders of the needier housewives of their neighborhood. Ellis's slightly shady business practices, plus a fortunate real estate transaction, made him enough additional money, despite some intervening setbacks, to bankroll his and Sarah's declining years.

The White Coffee Pot restaurant that I liked to go to with my parents was about a mile east of Grandpa Ellis's and Grandma Sarah's house on West North Avenue. One day while Ellis was driving to the slaughterhouse, he lost control of his car. The car jumped the curb and crashed through the plate glass window of the White Coffee Pot. As he sat in his car, his round, white-goateed face expressionless, the manager of the restaurant hurried out to see the cause of all the disarray and confusion. Seeing that Ellis was unhurt, he helped the old man on to a stool at the counter and asked him, sympathetically, if he could get him anything. To this Ellis, now a patron of the restaurant he just crashed into, is said to have replied in his rudimentary English, "Yeah, gimme cuppa' coffee."

4

THE NEIGHBORHOOD WITH NO NAME

"You can take the guy out of the neighborhood, but you can't
take the neighborhood out of the guy."

— Attributed to Frankie Valli

M Y NEIGHBORHOOD in the northwest quadrant of
Baltimore had no name then; to us, it was just "the
neighborhood." Many years later, when it was deemed deserving
of a name, it was granted its present-day designation, Woodbrook. My young life was largely circumscribed by its
three-by-two city block area: Auchentroly Terrace as the north-
east and northwest borders, Gwynns Falls Parkway as its
southeast boundary, and Reisterstown Road forming the south-
west line demarcating this diamond-shaped plot of city. Parallel
to, and between, Auchentroly Terrace and Reisterstown Road
ran two streets, Holmes Avenue and Woodbrook Avenue. Inter-
secting those two streets was just one street, Westbury Avenue,
its two blocks lying between Reisterstown Road and Holmes
Avenue. Behind each block of houses ran alleys that served as
access to the one-car garage behind each house, a place to put
out garbage cans for the garbage collectors to collect on
"garbage days," and a world of infinite possibilities for the
games the neighborhood boys played.

The Shaarei Tfiloh *shul* (synagogue), with its green-blue patinaed copper dome resting atop a classically Middle Eastern-style stone edifice, was the distinctive mark of my neighborhood. People from miles around were familiar with Shaarei Tfiloh because its striking architecture and location at the pinnacle of the small hill on which Holmes Avenue ran served as a memorable landmark. At the corner of Woodbrook Avenue and Auchentroly Terrace was the other neighborhood landmark, the Engine Company 52 firehouse. The kids in the neighborhood delighted in wandering over to the firehouse where the ever-tolerant firemen would let us gawk at their shiny red trucks and ask our silly questions ("Do you get hot fighting fires?", "What's it like sliding down the fire pole?") The engine house did indeed have a brass pole going from its second floor sleeping quarters to the ground floor, where the hose truck and hook-and-ladder truck waited to be called into service. These machines always gleamed, their gold lettering grandly proclaiming their station number. It gave the neighborhood kids a shot of pride to have such handsome machines right in *our* neighborhood. On the

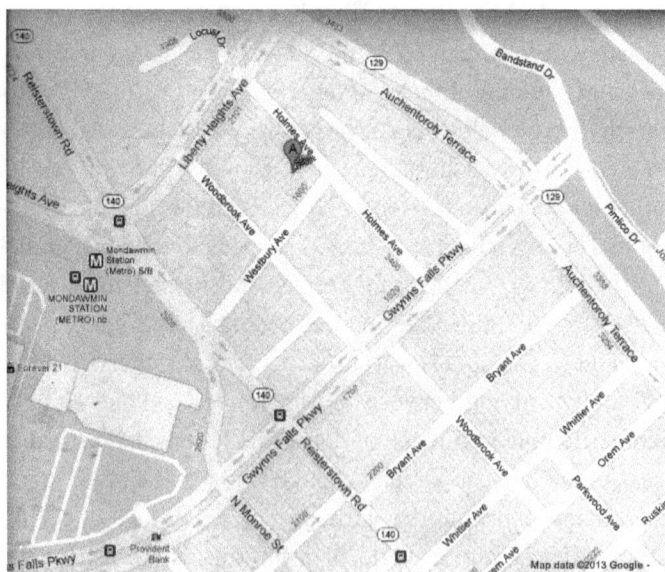

vacant lot next to the firehouse, the firemen planted a vegetable garden every summer. Across the street, in an apartment building overlooking Engine House 52, Neil Glasser lived. When the fire bell clanged to alert the resident firemen, Neil would be at the fire station before they could even open the doors to let the fire engines out. He remained an inveterate fire chaser for as long as he lived in the neighborhood (and probably even afterward).

In the map of the area as it is today, what's designated Liberty Heights Avenue was just a part of Auchentroly Terrace when I lived there.

We were fortunate to have, just beyond our neighborhood boundaries, a large urban park, Druid Hill Park. In it—all within walking distance of our house on Holmes Avenue—were the Baltimore Zoo, a boat lake, clay tennis courts, a plant conservatory, and a nice-sized hill that was great for sledding in the winter.

On the other side of our neighborhood boundaries was another attraction, looming as a ghostly presence adjacent to the neighborhood. Across Reisterstown Road stood a multi-acre fenced-in area we all called "Brown's Estate." No one in the neighborhood knew who Brown was, or whether this was even an apt name for the place, but that's what we called it. I later learned, as an adult, that it was the ancestral homestead of the merchant-banker Brown family in the 19th and early 20th centuries. It was undoubtedly built when the area was in the outer reaches of the city, but once the city crept up to it and then surrounded it in the 20th century, it stood as a mysterious oasis flanked by the city's roads and streets. No one I knew ever saw anyone go into or emerge from this mysterious place, and no one I knew ever ventured to climb the six-foot high, green-painted wooden fence surrounding it, for it was rumored among the neighborhood kids that vicious guard dogs patrolled its perimeter. It remained a place of endless fascination to us nonetheless. Sometimes at night we would venture across busy

Reisterstown Road just to see what we could see of this enig-
matic site, the braver among us being hoisted up by one of the
other kids to try to peer over the fence. The name an early
owner gave the place was Mondawmin. And many years later,
a shopping mall was developed on the site. Called Mondawmin
Mall (and in more recent times nicknamed "Murder Mall"), it
was labeled "Ground Zero" of the 2015 Baltimore unrest by
Johns Hopkins political scientist Lester Spence.

Our neighborhood was a homogeneous one, populated
mostly by first- or second-generation Jewish families. On our
side of the street lived the Lipnicks, Coltons, Kleins, Bergers,
Opels, and Wahrmans. On the other side of the street were
neighbors with last names like Hertzbach, Komins (probably
Kominski in the old country), Adler, Mandell, Taubenfeld,
Ochfeld, Rudo (probably Rudinsky in the old country), and
Kurland. Those Kurlands living directly across from us were
no relation to my mother's family, however. Kurland is a
common Jewish name that derives from the fact that in the 15th
through 17th century Jews were allowed to settle in the Duchy
of Courland, an area in Latvia west of the Dvina (now called
the Daugava) River. On the other streets in our neighborhood
lived the Greenfelds, Berkenfelds, Bernsteins, Millers, Gold-
bergs, Shapiros, Edelmans, and Rothschilds (no, not those
Rothschilds). Everyone in the neighborhood entered everyone
else's house without much ceremony. As a kid, I'd ring a doorbell, open the unlocked front door, and yell in, "Howard's
mother! Can Howard come out to play?"

I have always had a warm spot in my heart for babies and
infants. They are so innocent, cute, and cuddly, and smell so
nice (most of the time). One of the apartments in the house
next to ours was occupied, for a time, by a family with a baby
boy about 5 years younger than I. I would often ask Mrs. Levin
if I could play with Yale on their porch. He was a happy child
whom I enjoyed spending time with; when my little friend
moved away a few years later, I was greatly saddened and

missed him. I was reunited with him decades later when we came across one another after my mother's funeral. Yale was working at the restaurant where the after-funeral meal took place. It was like a bolt out of the blue to see him all grown up.

A year or two after Yale's family moved away from next door, my Uncle Len (my mother's youngest sibling) and Aunt Miriam moved into a house across the street and down the block from us. Uncle Len was born on Christmas day, 1921, just three years before my mother gave birth to my oldest brother, Leonard, making for an interesting uncle-nephew situation. My mother recalls that the day Uncle Len was born her father proclaimed to her and her siblings, in his Yiddish-accented English, "Guess vat Sendy Claus brought! A leettle baby brudder."

Uncle Len was straightforward, clear-thinking, and had a wry sense of humor; Aunt Min was vivacious, charming, and friendly. Together, they made a dynamic duo. Aunt Min often had our family over to join them for spaghetti and meat sauce dinners. My parents and siblings ate it up, so to speak. Picky eater that I was, I would ask Aunt Miriam to serve me the pasta without the meat sauce, and then I would pour ketchup over it before I ate it.

Whenever they needed me, I happily volunteered to baby sit their son, Geoffrey, who was about 5 years younger than I. Over the course of many baby-sits, I ended up anointing him with the nickname Godfrey Poodleby (don't ask me where that came from). Geoff was the little brother I didn't have.

———•◦•———

Uncle Len was a physician in the U.S. Public Health Service, which often required him and his family to move to new locations. When he was assigned to Phoenix, Arizona, a few years after he had moved across the street from us, he asked my parents if my brother Charlie and I could go with him and

Geoff on his drive to Phoenix, where he had to check on the progress of the house being built in anticipation of his move there. Charlie and I were delighted to go. We embarked on a two-week-long automobile trip across the northern tier of states on our way west, turning south in Wyoming for our ultimate destination, Phoenix. Did we ever see America on that trip! Niagara Falls, the Black Hills, Mount Rushmore, the Badlands, Great Salt Lake and Salt Lake City, and, of course, Phoenix. At a carnival in Wyoming, Charlie made quick friends with a cute carnie worker about his age. When we got to our motel for the night, Char borrowed Uncle Len's car to go back to see her— but that's a story you'll have to wait to read about if Charlie ever writes his memoir.

Uncle Len was a real stickler for planning and organization. He arranged the entire trip with what seemed to be precise minute-by-minute and stop-by-stop planning. In order to avoid time-consuming bathroom stops, Uncle Len drilled a hole in the floor of his old Hudson for us to pee in.

Uncle Len stayed in Phoenix with Geoff to take care of the arrangements he had driven there to see to. Charlie and I returned home by Greyhound bus, although we first took a bus west from Phoenix to Los Angeles to visit another uncle. Uncle Eddie, my mother's brother, and Aunt Julie had no children, but they always made a big to-do of their nieces and nephews. Uncle Eddie entertained us by taking us out to restaurants or lunches at poolside and into movie lots where he "fed the cattle," as he called the catering work for the film industry he did there. He was friends with Shemp Howard, one of the Three Stooges comedy team, and one day after we arrived in Los Angeles, he took us over to the Howards' home to meet Shemp. A large canasta game was in progress there. Shemp welcomed us warmly and invited teen-aged Charlie to sit in and play several hands (being a preteen, I hadn't learned yet how to play canasta). He ushered Charlie into the card room and politely pulled out a chair for Charlie to sit in. Charlie played for an hour with Shemp and his crowd, losing every hand. As we left, Charlie commented that he had never had such a bad run of luck at cards and couldn't understand how he could lose so consistently. Shemp just shrugged his shoulders and threw a mischievous gaze over to the chair Charlie had recently vacated and then to the large wall mirror behind the chair as the rest of the crowd at the table roared with laughter.

Our bus trip home from Los Angeles took us through the southern tier of the United States before veering north in Texas to return to Baltimore. We ate at roadside joints whenever the bus made a meal stop or at bus terminals. Once I discovered it on one of our meal stops, my favorite food order at the rest of those places was Southern style chicken-fried steak, smothered in gravy. I imagine I would exist today on a diet of chicken-fried steaks for dinner every night if I didn't mind doubling my weight every six months. During the trip, we slept on the bus as it drove through the night, with occasional breaks to stay in a motel. That was fairly easy for me; I could fall asleep at the drop of a hat just about anywhere. It was, I could tell, harder for Charlie, having to keep watch over his little brother and grabbing sleep whenever he could, but he kept his good humor throughout the whole trip.

Shortly after our homeward odyssey began, another passenger on the bus brought out a guitar, and pretty soon the whole bus was singing folk songs to while away the time. When we reached the Texas border, the bus driver stopped the bus and told our performer, sympathetically and in gentle terms, that he had to move to the back of the bus while we were passing through Texas. The black guitar player had no choice but to comply in spite of the pleadings of the other passengers to let him stay where he was. Fortunately, the guitar player was headed in the same direction we were, so we had his accompaniment for most of the way home. Would a whole busload of strangers singing in unison for days at a time still happen today? I wonder. Would a whole busload of strangers traveling in a bus today argue in unison against racial segregation?

———•———

Immediately to the south of our neighborhood was a block of stores on Reisterstown Road just south of Gwynns Falls Parkway: Wagner's Drug Store, Silber's Bakery, Paul's Delicatessen, Dogoloff's Grocery, and Sachs's Drug Store. Wagner's was where I went often for a coddie and a soda. Never heard of a coddie? Not to be confused with codfish cakes, a coddie was a uniquely Baltimore food consisting of salt cod fish mixed with potatoes, cracker meal, eggs, milk, pepper, and a few other ingredients, formed into a patty, coated with more cracker meal, and then deep-fried and served cold. One ate a coddie between crackers spread with mustard, often accompanied by a chocolate soda made at the soda fountain or a bottle of Almond Smash soda. Coddies sat out all day on the soda fountain counter. How they managed to be sold that way without anyone claiming to have become ill from eating them amazes me. Perhaps that's one reason I can still, in adulthood, eat food that is many days old without suffering ill effects—I've been immunized by coddies.

Silber's Bakery made, as their name implies, bread, cookies, pies, and cakes. It was the place where women of my mother's generation went to buy fresh-baked goods. Home baking was not for them because they took it as a sign that they had arrived economically if they could afford to buy store-made bakery goods. Whenever my mother anticipated someone coming to pay us a visit, she sent me or one of my siblings down to Silber's to buy cookies or a cake for the special guests, which my mother then proudly placed before them, being sure to mention the name of the bakery they came from. My favorites from Silber's were a cookie topped with a large dollop of chocolate ganache and a yellow layer cake frosted with chocolate.

Paul's Delicatessen sold lunch meats but also had a few tables for customers who wished to eat in. They had the best kosher hot dogs around—firm, a little spicy, and cooked just right. Their aroma permeated the place. It was near enough to where we lived that we could get a quick bite to eat if Mom or Dad wanted to treat us to something special nearby.

Prior to the era of supermarkets (Baltimore had only a few of those back then), we bought our groceries at the neighborhood grocery store. Dogoloff's had a cold-cuts counter and stocked canned items, some produce, and a few sundries. The present day is not the only era when resource conservation is encouraged. During the war (WWII, that is), in order to conserve paper "for the war effort," customers at Dogoloff's and other grocery stores had to bring in their previously-used paper bags for their purchases to be packed in.

Sachs Brothers' Drug Store was the hangout for the pre-teens and teens of our neighborhood. Yes, there were two drug stores on the same block. Both Sachs's and Wagner's sold over-the-counter drugs, prescription medicines, sundries, sodas, and coddies. But Sachs's had two things going for it that Wagner's did not, and those two things attracted the preadolescent and adolescent crowd: booths to sit in, rather than only the soda fountain stools that Wagner's had, and pinball machines.

I frequented Sachs's Drug Store so often that I can still envision its layout in my mind's eye. As you entered through its glass doors, a long soda fountain, with eight or nine stools, was on your right. Facing it, on your left, were four or five booths. A few fast, older girls—always dressed in tight sweaters and tight skirts—frequented Sachs's on occasion, claiming one of those booths, where they talked loudly about their late-night adventures with reefers and boys. They seemed to "adopt" us younger kids when we were there. The pre-teen boys like me would gather around them at their booth as they swapped their adventure tales with one another. Illicit drug use was almost unheard of in my growing-up years, so the tales these older girls told had a distinctly forbidden quality about them.

Farther left, beyond the booths, were shelves of over-the-counter drugs, notions, sundries, and whatnot. Continuing into the store toward the rear was the pharmacy counter. And just to the right of that, tucked into a far corner, was Valhalla—two nickel-a-play pinball machines of the latest manufacture that were almost always being played by someone. Sachs's paid off in cash for the wins pinball players racked up on the store's pinball machines. If you won some free games on one of the machines, you told one of Sachs's owners, brothers Ray and Milo Sachs, who then came by to verify your winnings and pay you a nickel for each game you racked up.

My newspaper delivery job for the *Baltimore-American* required me to collect money from my customers weekly. Since I bought the papers wholesale in advance from my route manager before delivering them, any money I collected from my customers was mine to keep, free and clear. The problem was that, flush with all those coins weighing heavily in my burlap collection pouch, I would often go to Sachs's after a morning of collecting and fritter away my earnings on the pinball machines. I somehow never won more money than I fed into those glamorous silver, wood, and glass monsters. It took me a while to learn to keep away from them if I were ever going to retain any of my paper route earnings.

———•———

Going to school at P.S. 60, on Francis Street and Clifton Avenue, meant leaving the neighborhood to go almost a mile south through another area that became more alien as I approached school, changing from predominantly Jewish to gentile and then to poor white (what we then called "hillbilly"). I've never been delivered to school in a school bus, for two reasons. The first was that we lived within a mile (just) of each of the elementary schools I attended, and the city did not provide transportation to students so situated. Second, beyond the elementary school level, Baltimore at that time did not provide school transportation no matter how far its students lived from their school. So, I either walked to P.S. 60 (usually not alone, but rather in packs with other kids from the neighborhood); walked three blocks to the trolley stop at the corner of Reisterstown Road and Gwynns Falls Parkway, got off at Fulton Avenue, and walked the remaining few blocks to school on Francis Street and Clifton Avenue; or went in the car with my father on those occasions when he could drop us off at school on his way to work.

On days we walked to school, we passed Moe's, a variety store on the corner of Woodbrook and Orem Avenues. Moe knew he had a potentially good customer base passing by daily, and he made sure to stock his cases and shelves with toys and candy to tempt the passing schoolchildren. My parents started me on an allowance of 25 cents a week to teach me how to budget, save, and spend wisely. Each time I stopped in to Moe's on my way to or from school raised an agonizing decision dilemma for me. Should I buy one of the wax fake lips I loved to wear and then chew, should I buy some tiny wax bottles filled with a divinely sweet liquid I similarly loved, or should I save my allowance for another time and a bigger treat (maybe an ice cream soda)? Echoing my parents' frugality, I did pretty well fostering my allowance, seldom blowing it the day I received it (my profligate spending of my paper route collection money came when I was a little older).

On one visit to Moe's I noticed an item he had just put out on the shelf: a silver-painted sword, just like the ones I saw in all the swashbuckler movies (except this one was made of rubber). This presented a real dilemma. The toy was no two-cent fake wax lips nor five-cent set of ambrosia-filled wax bottles. This was a toy that cost a full 98 cents. After viewing fondly this item for several days running, I took my dilemma to my parents. Should I spend all at once 98 cents of the money I had so conscientiously saved from my allowance in the biggest purchase of my young life up to then, I asked them, or should I pass this temptation by? Both my mother and father saw how I longed to own this sword, and they wisely counseled, "If you want it that much, it's okay to buy it." And I did.

———————

There was a more or less regular daily routine in the lives of the neighborhood kids. In the mornings during the school year, several of us gathered to walk or take the trolley to school, and in the afternoons after school we gathered on little-trafficked Westbury Avenue to begin our round of street games—more about those in a later chapter—until it was time to go home for supper. In the evenings in the winter, we would be inside doing our homework, listening to the radio, or more often, both. On summer nights, once school was out for the year, we played street or alley games, sat out on our concrete stoops to take in the night air, talked to neighbors, caught lightning bugs, or looked up at the stars. My father was particularly taken with stargazing. He vividly recalled seeing, when he still lived in the old country in 1910, Halley's Comet and being awed by it. Often on nights after he came home from work, we would go outside to look up at the stars together and marvel at how far they were from us and from each other. It boggled his and my minds, and it still does mine.

One summer, William D. McElroy and Emil H. White, eminent researchers at Johns Hopkins University, offered a bounty on lightning bugs. The Hopkins researchers were studying the characteristics of luciferin, the compound responsible for the lightning bugs' ability to produce light. Knowing that local kids liked to catch and release them to watch them light up harmlessly in their hands, they recruited swarms of Baltimore children to collect lightning bugs for their research. Since I engaged in the capture and release of the little insects anyway, I just continued that summer capturing them, but putting them in bottles instead of letting them loose. In that way, I earned a few dollars for an activity I normally did for free.

During the summer, families solved the problem of Baltimore's hot, muggy nights by spending time outside, where whatever breeze there might be could find us. Air conditioning was something you only found in some movie theaters. Not in the streetcars, not in the schools, and certainly not in houses in the 1940s unless you were rich. Sitting on our front steps, we took in the cooler night air and talked among ourselves or with neighbors. Sometimes we'd take a radio outside, string an extension cord to a plug inside the house, and listen to radio suspense dramas. Television? That was something only better-off people were beginning to acquire and, because it seemed to be radio with pictures, was to me a source of amazement when I first heard about it.

My bedroom being at the front of our house, I could look down from my bed onto the street and to the neighbors' houses across the way. The Komins family lived on the opposite side of the street from us. They were the first family on our street to purchase one of those new sensations, a television set. I often propped myself up on my bed and peered out the window at their living room as the lights from their television set flashed brightly, then dimly, then brightly again, and shafts of light moved across their window panes. I would regularly look at this light show and wonder what this new marvel would reveal if only I could actually see it.

Finally, one evening after going up to bed and watching the television flicker across the way in the Komins's windows, I could withstand the agony no further. I went downstairs and asked my mother if I could go across the street to ask the Kominses if they would let me watch their television. "Only this once," my mother cautioned. I hurriedly changed out of my pajamas, went across the street, and rang their doorbell. Mrs. Komins welcomed me in after I told her the reason for my visit. That evening's exposure to television had to satisfy me until I could cadge some other television viewing at the houses of other people who, as time went on, acquired a television set. Eventually, a few years later, my parents bought our own black-and-white light-emitting wonder. Our family had reached the television age.

When it came time to go to bed, my siblings and I had a way of remaining outside to sleep if the temperature had been extremely warm during the day. Two ways, actually. One was to walk over to Druid Hill Park and sleep in the park. That's right, sleep in the park. In those days at the end of World War II and beyond, people could lie down on the grass to sleep in the park unmolested by either muggers or the Park Police. Muggers was a term I never even heard of until many years later. The Park Police seemed to accept the fact that, in Baltimore's sticky summers, people took to sleeping in the park, and they left them alone. The second way to beat the heat was to sleep in the rear screened-in porch on the second floor of our house. There we would set up our canvas cots and throw sheets over them, providing places for three of us to sleep in cool comfort. Our parents, whose room was right next to the door leading to the screened porch, never slept out there with us. I don't recall how we solved the problem of choosing who would get a cot to sleep on if four or all five of the kids wanted to sleep there at the same time, but somehow we worked it out.

The streets were not dead during the day while the neighborhood children were in school. A vital and active street scene went on as a regular contingent of peddlers of various kinds came around offering goods and services. At a time when most families had only one car—and some had none—many of the necessities of life would come to you rather than you to them. Street hucksters announced their presence each in their own distinctive way, and if you wanted what they had to offer, you just went down the front steps to the street to buy it.

The scissors man came walking down the street once a month, pushing his grinding wheel cart before him, ringing the bell mounted on its front, yelling "Scissors" to announce his presence. If you had scissors, knives—even hatchets—that were dull, the scissors man could put as keen an edge as ever would be seen on them. The fish lady needed no bell nor yell to announce her presence; in fact, I don't recall ever hearing her talk. She just showed up at your house, if you were one of her customers, every Thursday morning with her wicker basket layered with fish of various stripes (so to speak), each layer cushioned by newspaper. She seemed to be as old as my grandmothers were. I watched with fascination as this old woman made her way up and down the street to serve her customers, her gray hair pulled back in a bun, her bowlegs stretching to their maximum as she walked-ran faster than most men half her age could sprint.

Which came first, the chicken or the egg? I don't know, but we had access to both in our neighborhood. A peddler would often come with wooden cages containing live chickens he would kill for you if you were so inclined. We were not, as we obtained our chicken and other meat from my grandfather's butcher shop, but some of our neighbors patronized the poultry man. The egg man came along in a truck and took your order one week and came back to your door the next with the order of eggs he had gathered for you that morning from his farm in "the country."

Another visitor by truck from the country was the milkman, he on a regular daily basis. He knew your dairy wants and needs without having to ask and left your order in an insulated metal box on your porch. If you needed to change your regular dairy order on occasion, you left him a note in the milk box and he'd accommodate the change. The milk came in glass bottles and, unless you especially ordered homogenized milk, which was seldom the case, the top fifth of the bottle contained the cream that settled out on top of the milk. On particularly cold winter days, the insulated box notwithstanding, the cream at the top might freeze, expand, and pop the top if the milk wasn't taken into the house in a timely fashion.

"Watermelllohn, red to de rahnd! You pick it, I'll plug it." That song, sung by street A-rabs, with the clopping of horses' hooves keeping the beat, meant that the wagon was coming around with watermelons right off the boats of Baltimore harbor. As written in the *Baltimore Sun* newspaper, by long-standing convention in Baltimore a street peddler operating a horse-drawn cart of fresh produce is called an *A-rab*, pronounced *AY-rab* in Baltimorese. When I heard the watermelon peddler's cry, my mouth would start to water, and I'd yell to my mother— just in case she hadn't heard—that the watermelon man was here. I'd follow her down our concrete steps to the street and watch as she stopped at the wagon, thumped several of the brightest, biggest, most verdant fruits sitting in it, and then solemnly pointed. "Plug this one," she'd say. She'd hold the newly cut wedge the watermelon man had cut for her close to her face, eyeing it as if she were about to taste a glass of fine red wine. If it passed her inspection, she'd pay the man for the watermelon, while I offered to help her bring it up the steps—with the expectation, of course, that I would get the first taste as my reward. If it didn't pass muster, she'd tell the "sommelier" that this one didn't look good and to please plug another "fine wine" for examination.

Mr. Goldberg, whom my parents endearingly termed "the huckster," came not by foot, not by horse-drawn wagon, but by truck, announcing his presence with the *oogah* of his truck's horn. Its open rear bed was loaded with every manner of fruit and vegetable. Onions, he had them. Carrots, by the bunch. Apples, sure. Customers picked what they wanted, Mr. Goldberg weighed it out on the scale at the back of his truck, the customers paid him, and produce shopping was done for another few days.

Even the alleys behind the rows of houses were scenes of commerce of a sort. Junk men (or rag pickers—take your pick of terminology) would come into the alleys at irregular intervals, either driving a horse and wagon or pushing a cart. They would poke around the garbage cans out back looking for pieces of glass, metal, fabric, wire and other scrap they would aggregate and ultimately sell. The original recyclers, they were.

Every once in a while in the summer months, a man leading a small pony came by and asked the residents if they wanted to have their child's photo taken sitting on the pony—for a price, of course. In the midst of the city, it was like having "the country" brought to you to enjoy, if only for a moment. So there I am, three years old, sitting atop a pony in front of our house looking none too happy. The pony's pale mane and black splotches on his white body stand out. The sun seems to be shining so brightly that everything looks fresh and clean.

Another regular summer visitor adding to the street scene was Al, the Good Humor ice cream man. He announced his arrival on our street by jingling the bells atop his white refrigerated truck. On hearing the daily jingle—twice daily in the thick of summer—kids poured out of their houses to buy the popsicles, creamsicles, and chocolate-covered Good Humor

bars Al, always dressed in a white shirt, bowtie, and pants, sold. I never knew another Good Humor man in our neighborhood but Al. His job was his only job, apparently, and he stayed with it all through my childhood.

Two other regulars visited our street, visitors of a type virtually unknown to people today. Early every evening, the lamplighter came along carrying a ladder to light manually the gas lamps that provided the yellowish street lights of "warmth and welcome," as one newspaper's nostalgia article put it, that illuminated the neighborhoods of Baltimore. He'd take the ladder from his shoulder, place it against the lamppost, climb up to the glass lamp enclosure and lift it, then light the mantle in the lamp and climb back down. The following morning, he'd come along to each lamppost and climb the ladder again to extinguish the light. "At the end of World War II, there were some 16,000 gas lamps still in operation in Baltimore. By the early 1950s, when Mayor Thomas D'Alesandro began conversion of the city's lighting to mercury vapor lamps, there were still more than 10,000 gas lamps casting their wonderful soft, yellow-greenish light across the city," that same October 10, 1998 *Baltimore Sun* newspaper article reported. Nowadays, if you come across an old street lamp in some cities' "nostalgia" quarters, odds are it is a surplus Baltimore street lamp from the 1940s.

Mr. Johnson, the city policeman, walked his beat past our house at least a couple of times a day, twirling his nightstick with practiced fluidity. Like Al, the Good Humor man, he held his job as a beat cop for almost as long as I lived in the neighborhood. I was fascinated by the gun he carried in his holster, and I often engaged him in conversation about the dangerous piece of equipment that hugged his waist. Making friends with the residents, Mr. Johnson knew us all by name, and his presence reassured us that peace would prevail in the neighborhood—and it did. In the early 1950s, though, the Baltimore Police Department changed its policy, and police cars began making the rounds of the neighborhoods. In my mind, they could not replace Mr. Johnson's knowledge of the neighborhood's denizens nor his interactions with the community the police were sworn to protect.

There was a whole sound and look to the street life in the Baltimore of my youth that's no longer alive in urban America today. Our lives are more streamlined and our streets now sound different. There's an ineffable something—a certain noise, a distinctive song—missing from them both. "*Oogah, oogah!*" "*Jingle, jingle!*" "Watermelllohn, red to de rahnd!"

As I entered my teen years, the area just to the south of us became increasingly populated with black families. As they moved in and up, the whites moved out, a common pattern in America's cities in the '40s, '50s, and '60s. My parents were no exception to this trend, but until they did make that move out, I was pals with several of the black kids. One of them, Cookie, claimed to be a cousin of one of the Ink Spots—the Ink Spots, the most famous singing group in America at the time! *If I Didn't Care* and *I Don't Want to Set the World on Fire* were two of their big hits. I just couldn't believe that someone I actually knew was related to a member of that famous singing group I had heard so often on the radio, and I challenged Cookie to prove the veracity of his claim of familial relationship. To prove it, he invited me up to his apartment on Reisterstown Road. There, on his family's piano, stood a framed, signed photo of the group. Since Bill Kenny, the best-known member of the quartet, was from Baltimore, I didn't doubt the truth of what Cookie was telling me. I was a believer after that.

One day, when I was 14, my mother told me we were going to move to a new house "farther out." I knew the reason why and objected mightily. To my mind, our old house and old neighborhood served us well and comfortably, and it was the only neighborhood I knew or could imagine living in. When it came to race, I had absorbed the lessons the teachers at my elementary school, segregated though it was, tried to instill in their students—that there was no reason to dislike others who were different from you. My parents, the children of their own generation and their own history, received no such lessons, and in their mind, although they did not hate blacks, they did not want to live next to them, either.

So my family participated in the white flight that characterized major urban areas of the time and moved farther out to 3707 Cold Spring Lane, about halfway between our old neighborhood and the city limits. It was a fully detached, two-story brick and wood house with a short driveway leading off the street on which to park one's car—a big step up from the attached row house with an alley and garage in the back that was my home base for my whole life until then. Of course, my parents made the second floor of this new house into an apartment for tenants, but this time they installed an outside flight of stairs so the tenants could access it without having to come through our house—another big step up. The downstairs had two bedrooms in it, and since by then all my brothers and sister had married and moved away, our first floor could readily accommodate my parents and me—and me in a bedroom I didn't have to share with anyone.

The tenants my parents attracted to this new apartment in our house were a lot more interesting to me than the ones who lived in our old house. The first tenant was a full-blooded Mohawk Indian who, like many of his tribal confreres, worked in high elevation iron and steel. He had moved to Baltimore from New York for job reasons. I delighted in hearing his stories about the skyscrapers in his home state he had worked on and how he moved from beam to beam, with no safety harness to impede him, 30 floors above street level. After he moved away, Len Towne, an engineer, also from New York, moved into the apartment above us, also for job-related reasons. Len took a liking to me and sought to widen the horizons of the naïve 15-year-old son of his landlords. Our frequent chats included his asking me about my plans for the future, encouraging me to follow my dreams, and giving me his views on how life really was. Often, he shared with me a recounting of his numerous adventures with the ladies, of which he had many. I was eager to learn from him, to correct the misinformation I recognized I was getting from my buddies and to confirm the few facts I thought to be true. Len, in turn, was eager to oblige to move my development in that area along. I knew he was speaking from experience. Young as I was, I could put two and two together to conclude that the women he brought to his apartment upstairs were not up there to have tea. I don't think my parents noticed the bevy of beauties that regularly tromped up the outside stairs with our tenant Len, but I sure did.

By the time we had moved from Holmes Avenue, I was far enough along in high school and busy with schoolwork and extracurricular activities that I ended up not missing my old stomping grounds as much as I thought I would. At that point, too, with all my siblings married, I was no longer surrounded by my brothers and sister. Living in the new house, in a new neighborhood, with just my parents and me in it—after a full house of seven for the first fourteen years of my life—was a different experience from before. But in a way, the old neighborhood was so much a part of me that I carried it with me for the rest of my life, no matter where I lived or how old I became.

5

THE WAR

"Today we know that World War II began not in 1939
or 1941 but in the 1920's and 1930's when those who should
have known better persuaded themselves that they
were not their brother's keeper."
— Hubert H. Humphrey

ALMOST EVERYONE just called it "The War," for anyone younger than 35 at the time had no memory or experience of the earlier world war. The drumbeat for World War II started in the 1930s as Chancellor Adolf Hitler led the German people into ever more aggressive actions against Germany's neighbors, conquering Czechoslovakia and annexing Austria early in 1939 and invading Poland a few months later. The United States held back entering into war until it no longer could. The nation formally entered World War II the day after the Japanese conducted a devastating sneak attack on the U.S. base at Pearl Harbor in Hawaii. "Yesterday, December 7th, 1941—a date which will live in infamy—" President Franklin D. Roosevelt intoned before Congress in his stentorian, patrician voice, "the United States of America was suddenly and deliberately attacked by naval and air forces of the Empire of Japan." He concluded his speech by asking Congress formally to declare war: "Hostilities exist. There is no blinking at the fact that our people, our territory, and our interests are in grave danger. With confidence in our armed forces, with the unbounding determination of our people, we will gain the inevitable triumph—so help us God. I ask that the Congress declare that since the unprovoked and dastardly attack by Japan on Sunday, December 7th, 1941, a state of war has existed between the United States and the Japanese empire."

His clarion call to Congress that day was also a clarion call to the people of the country. The war permeated every family's thoughts and actions in ways big and small. Suddenly, men of military age were disappearing from neighborhoods across the country, leaving to serve in the armed forces. Small white flags with one or several stars on them began appearing in house windows indicating the family had a "boy" or "boys" in the service.

My brother Leonard was exempt from being drafted because of his polio-affected arm and his lack of vision in one eye, although he tried to pass the draft physical by memorizing the eye chart. Being refused enlistment, he looked for another way to aid the war effort and show his loyalty to the country that provided us with the opportunities it did. For part of the war years, he worked in a defense plant, the Glenn L. Martin aircraft manufacturer in Baltimore, a major defense industry player at that time. The rest of the boys in our family were too young to be drafted. But the war was a big thing in all our lives nonetheless. In my life, in particular, it was a looming presence for the entire first six years of my life.

It was both an exciting and a fearful time, especially for a child as young as I was. It was widely believed that our American homeland could experience bombs falling on us. Coastal cities conducted air raid drills, during which every house had to shut off its lights and pull down its window shades. Air raid wardens went about our neighborhood to ensure that all houses followed the rules. At school, too, we conducted similar drills, with teachers leading us into supposedly safe parts of the school building. These were not empty exercises. Although the odds were small that Germany or Japan could deliver bombs effectively to the continental United States, our enemies' technologies were being developed to make long-range bombing of the American homeland a possibility.

Indeed, in a little-remembered incident, a year after Pearl Harbor the Japanese conducted a test in which they catapulted a float plane from a submarine off the coast of Oregon. The plane dropped two incendiary bombs into a heavily forested area. The aim of this bombing was to start forest fires along our west coast. Fortunately, they did not factor in Oregon's coastal fog, mist, and rain, which made the forest too damp to catch fire. A few years later, Japan implemented a more workable, though still unsuccessful, scheme. That program sent up torrents of balloons from Japan carrying incendiary bombs into the jet stream, which were released once they were over the U.S. Although thousands of bombs were sent up this way, and a good portion of them exploded in the northwestern quadrant of the United States and southwestern part of Canada, they did little strategic damage because they lacked targeting capability.

As kids, we played war games, using broomsticks, boards, and our fingers as guns as we pretended being soldiers in the war facing the Japs or Germans in battle. Firing at our imaginary enemies or tossing imaginary hand grenades, all accompanied by the appropriate self-produced "ptoo" of the gunshots and "brroom" of the grenade explosions, we fought battles—and usually won them. Movie theaters regularly showed newsreels as part of their fare, and a common part of every newsreel during the war consisted of scenes shot from wing-mounted cameras showing air battles with Japanese planes over the Pacific or our planes strafing German trains on the ground. I joined loudly in the cheers of "Get those damn Japs" or "Give them Nazis hell!" that went up in the darkened theater as our airmen put to the torch the Japanese Zeroes they engaged or the luckless German trains unfortunate enough to catch the fire of "our boys."

During World War II, the Army camps in Baltimore's environs (Fort Meade, Fort Holabird) housed German prisoners of war. Whenever our car, on one of our family's occasional weekend country jaunts, passed a group of these POWs congregating near a fence along the road, my siblings and I hurriedly cranked down the windows and started singing loudly *Der Fuehrer's Face*, a song made popular by the Spike Jones Band. The song parodied the Nazi anthem, *The Horst Wessel Song*, and derogated the Nazis:

Ven der Fuehrer says,
'Ve ist der master race'
Ve Heil!{boo} Heil!{boo}
Right in Der Fuehrer's face.

We thought it was hilarious to taunt those lousy Germans in that manner. The POWs, for their part, probably didn't understand the lyrics and were glad just to be out of the fighting and getting three squares a day in decent surroundings.

As the U.S. economy shifted to war production, meat, sugar, butter, gasoline, and other necessities were rationed because they were needed to support the war effort. Families were issued ration cards for these commodities by the U.S. Office of Price Administration. Schools conducted scrap drives to collect material to help the war effort. I was driven to school often with bales of newspapers my friends and I had collected, dropping them off at the collection point in front of the school. Then I stood around with my schoolmates as we watched the collection of bundled papers grow as others came and did the same until the piles reached from one end of the school building to the other. At other times, we brought in scrap metal—cans, old wheels, and the like—for the scrap metal drives that helped the war effort. We also helped by saving our paper bags from the grocery store and bringing them back to the store for subsequent purchases to be placed in. Recycling is not a new phenomenon.

Schoolchildren even contributed financially to the war cause by buying, in school, savings bond stamps for a few cents each. We pasted these stamps into a special book, and when we had pasted the stamps in all the spots in the book, we traded the book in for an actual U.S. War Bond, the proceeds of which went to finance the war effort.

It all came to an end in the spring and summer of 1945. On May 8th, the day after German General Jodl signed the unconditional surrender document that formally ended war in Europe, V.E. Day (Victory in Europe Day) was declared. Hitler's vaunted "Thousand Year Reich" had lasted a mere 12 years. On August 15, after an atomic bomb was dropped on Hiroshima on August 6th and another fell on Nagasaki three days later because the Japanese still had not capitulated, V.J. Day (Victory in Japan Day) was declared. Although it wasn't until September 2nd that Japan signed the instrument of surrender on the deck of the battleship U.S.S. Missouri in Tokyo Bay, battle-weary America started celebrating even before the instrument of surrender was signed. So momentous was that "official" event, marking as it did the formal close of the second of the two theaters of war we were engaged in, facsimiles of the surrender document were immediately produced for sale. My family bought one.

The war was over, and people on the home front rejoiced like never before. Spontaneously, but as if on an invisible signal, on V.J. Day everyone in our neighborhood went onto their porches to celebrate the end of war. Up and down the row of houses on Holmes Avenue, we and our neighbors beat pots and pans with spoons, spun noisemakers, or just cheered. That night, my brother Charlie and sister Margie took me downtown with them to another spontaneous celebration. Thousands and thousands of people—more people than I had ever been among at any one time—thronged the area around Lexington and Howard Streets in the center of Baltimore's downtown shopping district. There, amid the major downtown department stores—Hutzler's, the Hecht Company, Stewarts, Hochschild, Kohn, and Company—people of all ages laughed and screamed that the war was over. Anyone in uniform was mobbed, kissed, and hoisted onto the crowd's shoulders.

It was bedlam but a well-mannered bedlam. Everyone was in the best of moods. The thoughts in everyone's minds were that peace was finally at hand, our soldiers who had survived battle were coming home, rationing soon would be over, and we could get back to living more or less normal lives. And, gradually over the immediately ensuing years, that's what happened. Ration books and saving stamp books were no longer needed, film footage of dog fights with the enemy stopped appearing in the newsreels, young men who had been in the military and were fortunate enough to have survived were welcomed back home, and peace seemed to be at hand. Since I had no memory of anything before the war, I couldn't say that it was just like prewar years, but not having the war in our lives lent a distinctly different air to everyday living, even to a six-year-old like me.

For several years afterward, there remained a lingering everyday reminder of the war. At the end of the war, the government was left with a huge stockpile of khaki-colored paint that had been used to paint tanks, jeeps, anti-aircraft guns, and other war materiel. Following the wartime practice of not wasting any resource, soon all U.S. Post Office trucks and mailboxes were painted khaki. These provided daily reminders, wherever you turned, that the war was over yet not forgotten. It was some years—into the 1950s—before all the surplus paint was used up and the postal service was free to adopt its more cheerful and meaningful red, white, and blue colors for its trucks and mailboxes.

During the war, I heard vague talk about concentration camps in Germany holding Jews within their barbed wire fences, but little solid information about that was released to the public. The full picture did not come out until the death camps were liberated by allied forces at the end of the war and the subsequent trials at Nuremberg revealed the extent of the atrocities the Germans visited upon Jews, Gypsies, homosexuals, and other "inferior" peoples. In the years immediately after World War II ended, unfamiliar grown-ups began to appear here and there in our neighborhood. To my young eyes, they were alien people who seemed to have fallen mysteriously from the sky to alight in our presence. They stayed with distant relatives in our neighborhood, spoke with heavy European accents, and had indigo-colored numbers tattooed on their pale forearms. They were the survivors of the German death camps, displaced Jews who were lucky to be alive but who had lost their homes, livelihood, and close family relatives and had to start all over again in a new and strange land across the sea. They stayed for a while with these distant relatives until they found living and working situations, and then they faded away. My family didn't know any of them personally, but their mysterious appearance in, and then equally quiet disappearance from, our neighborhood was another way the end of World War II is marked in my memory.

6

SCHOOL DAZE

". . . if one advances confidently in the direction of his
dreams, and endeavors to live the life
which he has imagined, he will meet with
a success unexpected in common hours. . . ."
— Henry David Thoreau, *Walden*

I CHOSE THE HACKNEYED title and spelling of this
chapter heading deliberately. I sailed through the greater
part of my education in a bit of a daze. I didn't have much sense
of self to begin with and was at the whim of circumstance and
the influence of others. Several winds especially were pushing
at my back in those early school years. The first was the influence
of my family. My parents valued education highly, and my
brothers and sister set examples for me of industriousness,
studiousness, and achievement. They all were conscientious students, skipping grades and graduating high school at a younger
age than their peers. Second, my mother made most of the decisions about the direction of my education and life. Now, no one
would expect a callow youth to have the knowledge and life
experience to make important decisions by himself. But at all
the important decision points, I was not even consulted by my
mother; rather, I was presented pretty much with *faits accomplis*.

The third wind at my back during that time was the simple fact that learning new things was easy for me, as well as exciting. In that way, those years sped by. I didn't have to exert much effort; I just sailed through. Mom loved to tell the story of the time I came home from second grade one day with my friend Howard. As we walked in the door, she asked us, "So, well, what did you learn in school today?" "Nuthin' much," was Howard's reply. I, on the other hand, regaled her with a full narrative about how we learned the "sevens" multiplication tables, that sentences have both a subject and a verb, and on and on for 10 minutes.

Once I reached college, I experienced another kind of daze, the daze that comes from learning a whole raft of new things and having new worlds open to me in a rush. By the time I entered Johns Hopkins University at the age of 15, I was beginning (albeit only beginning) to gain a better sense of myself and what I might want to do with my life. I entered with the possibility that I might want to major in psychology. I was interested in what made people tick, what made one person take one approach to life and another, a different one, and, especially, how people come to develop the way they perceive the world.

————•◆•————

I turned five years old in January 1944, and in February, I entered kindergarten in Public School 60. In that era, Baltimore had two public school entrance months, February and September, and a child entered kindergarten in the one closest to his or her fifth birthday. My enrollment in P.S. 60 was foreordained, as you went to the elementary school closest to your neighborhood. Considering a private school education was not even in the realm of thinking of anyone I knew—only "rich people" could afford such a thing, and no one we knew was in that boat. In fact, it was only when I entered college that I became acquainted with anyone who had gone to a private school.

My kindergarten teacher at P.S. 60 was Ceil Mannheimer, a strapping woman who appeared to my young eyes to be in her 50s. Miss Mannheimer (all our female teachers were "Miss," whether married or not) kept us busy cutting out construction paper and gluing it to other construction paper, drawing, and "learning our letters." She also kept the classroom constantly entertained by passing gas freely and noisily with little regard for what her young charges might think of the practice.

For first grade, I had Miss Lulu Ellingsworth, a lovely, gentle lady. My principal memory of her is that her wrinkled face, gray hair, and bird-like figure made her appear ancient to six-year-old me. After a year of learning the rudiments of the three Rs in Miss Ellingsworth's first grade, I passed from there into Miss Dacy's second grade. Miss Dacy was known around the school for three things: wearing heavy white makeup on her face, wearing a wig (it was rumored), and requiring misbehaving students to sit under her desk as punishment while she sat there teaching the rest of the class. The boys in our class had a grand time twittering and talking in whispers about what you could see looking up Miss Dacy's dress if she consigned you (as I once was consigned) to under-desk punishment. The tops of her thighs were whiter than white, I confidently reported to my friends based on that subterranean view.

The street on which my elementary school was located, Francis Street, was home to the infamous Francis Streeters. The Francis Streeters, as I've already suggested, were a gang of what my parents called "hillbillies" (families that had moved to the "big city" from Virginia, West Virginia, North Carolina, and points south) who lived around Francis Street, Clifton Avenue, and Fulton Avenue. These kids specialized in anti-Semitic slurs and physical harassment, up to and including beating, of any Jewish kids who happened their way.

Although my own contacts with the Francis Streeters were not all that frequent (I was advised energetically and often to avoid them if at all possible, advice to which I tried to adhere), my memories of them are vivid. One day, as I was walking to P.S. 60 by myself, I turned the corner to come face-to-face with a terrified boy running in my direction, pursued by three Francis Streeters. One of the gang held a manual can opener, the kind with a sharp metal point at the end of a wooden handle. The kid being chased was running so fast, and I was so taken by surprise, that I could not make out who he was. The pursuing Francis Streeters were so intent on running the boy down that they did not stop to check me out. I think I was too small a fish to be of much challenge or interest to them, anyway. That I did not hear afterward of anyone being grievously injured makes me think that the boy being pursued ran faster and longer than his pursuers.

At the end of second grade, a decision I didn't participate in was made about my schooling. My mother was concerned that P.S. 60 was located in such a tough neighborhood that I might come to harm, so she arranged for me to be transferred to Public School 18, located on Druid Park Drive in a distinctly better area about a mile in the other direction from my house than P.S. 60 was. I entered the third grade of P.S. 18 in Selma Meyerson's class, but a funny thing happened on the way to Miss Meyerson's. It turned out that, at that time, my oldest brother Leonard, who was then 22, was dating Miss Meyerson, an attractive woman with alluring red tresses whose nickname to her grown-up friends was Pepe. Leonard brought her home after a date one evening, and somehow I ended up sitting on her lap. Maybe she thought that having Leonard's youngest brother cuddle up to her might ingratiate herself to Len and our family. Hell, whatever the reason, I didn't mind: I was in seventh heaven. I reported this all enthusiastically to my new classmates the next time I was in school, including the fact, little-known to my classmates, that her nickname was Pepe. "Nah, you're making that up. No teacher goes into her pupils' houses. And I betcha her name ain't Pepe, either" was the kind of response my report drew from my classmates and friends. But, ah, I knew, I knew.

Whether or not it was Miss Meyerson's (short-term) relationship with my brother, or the fact that I had come home from first and second grades with mostly "Excellents" on my report card, or the fact that I was a February-entering student and therefore out of kilter with the majority September-entering school population, I was soon "skipped" (advanced) out of the second half of third grade into Mr. Berensohn's fourth grade class. Mr. Berensohn was that rare phenomenon at the time: a male elementary school teacher. He and the fifth-grade teacher, Miss Demerowski, were seen frequently talking together in the hallways of the school, giving rise to whispered rumors (whether true or not, I don't know) among the pupils of P.S. 18 that they were romantically linked. By the time I finished Miss Brooks's sixth grade class at P.S. 18, I had been skipped two more half grades, amounting to being advanced through P.S. 18 by a total of one-and-a-half years. Although I had no trouble keeping up each time I was placed in another half-grade ahead of me, I retain to this day gaps in areas of my knowledge that I am sure came about because of the grades I skipped in elementary school. I still cannot identify many parts of speech with their correct names and do not know many of the rules of grammar well enough to express them clearly, among other failings.

Recesses at P.S. 18 were a lot better than the recesses at P.S. 60, I recall. The school yard at P.S. 18 was much larger and more open than that of P.S. 60, and it had grass in it, unlike the small, brick-surfaced recess yard of P.S. 60. We could run around a lot more energetically at my new school than in my former school's more confined space. But the thing I remember most about the P.S. 18 recesses was that we were visited often by men who would demonstrate (and try to sell us) the latest model yo-yos. These men (almost all of them Filipino) would dazzle us with demonstrations of the terrific tricks their brand of yo-yo was capable of. The school children would stop what they were doing during recess and gather around these diminutive yo-yo demonstrators as they dazzled us with tricks like "around the world," "walking the dog," "rocking the baby," and "bite my cuff."

———•─•──

The next phase of my education, junior high school, consisted of grades seven through nine. Because of where I lived, I was slated to enter P.S. 79, a junior high school located closer in to the center of the city and with a reputation for having a rough student body (a reputation confirmed by Charlie, who spent his junior high school years there). The regular initiation rite for new boys at P.S. 79 was for the older students to grab them in the boys' recess yard and toss them over the 6-foot-high wooden fence into the girls' recess yard. The girls were so tough they sometimes picked the newbie off the ground and tossed him back over the fence into the boys' recess yard.

There was one public junior high school, however, that was open city-wide, but by invitation only. Public School 49 was a junior high school for what would now be called gifted and talented students. It had an accelerated curriculum whereby students were moved through the three junior high school grades in two years instead of three. Students were admitted only by their grade school teachers' recommendations for admittance. I was recommended for it, and that is where I spent grades seven, eight, and nine.

As a physical plant, Robert E. Lee Junior High School, Number 49, was no great shakes, housed as it was in an old brick town house on Cathedral Street near West Mount Royal Avenue. It had no auditorium and no labs. Across the brick courtyard behind it that served as the recess yard was a former stable that served as the school's gym. The cafeteria of the school was in its mostly windowless basement nestled among steam pipes and other basement equipment. Today, that dank, dimly lit cafeteria would probably not pass muster as a place for the hygienic preparation and serving of food. Not that it would have made any difference to me, as Mom always packed a lunch for me all the way through high school and even into college (it was cheaper than buying lunch at the cafeteria). But the education School 49 offered its smart and motivated students was first-rate.

My homeroom teacher there was Miss Dann, but the teacher I remember most vividly was Olga Bawden, who taught French. Miss Bawden swept into my first day of seventh-grade French class saying, "Bonjour, mes élèves. Asseyez-vous et ouvrez vos livres." No one in the class understood what she said, but it was clear that we would have to learn fast if we were to get anything out of the class. For the next two years, I never heard Miss Bawden speak a word of English inside that classroom. Although those two years with Miss Bawden when I was a preteen were my only instruction in French, to this day, more than half a century later, I retain a rudimentary ability to speak and understand French, so long as it's spoken slowly enough for me to "get" it. I am all for immersion learning of languages.

To take the manual arts classes that were part of the curriculum in junior high school, the boys walked through the park adjacent to the Mt. Royal Train Station to a group of permanent "portable" buildings for our shop classes in electricity, sheet metal, and the like. For their classes in home economics, the girls walked a little farther on to nearby School 79.

Mr. Jaffe taught algebra and taught it clearly and well, and there were other teachers whose names I no longer remember who also provided a solid education for me and the other P.S. 49 students. But Miss Bawden is the one whose teaching and teaching style are burned into my memory.

Once I graduated from 49 in '51, I entered high school at Baltimore Polytechnic Institute, and the next seven years of my education, until I entered graduate school, took place in all-male environments. My entrance into Poly was foreordained by family momentum: all three of my brothers had gone there. An all-boys high school then, it had a rigorous curriculum with a strong emphasis on math, science, and technical subjects. Many of its students went on to study engineering in college, no doubt influenced by Poly's curriculum. Dr. Wilmer DeHuff was Poly's hands-on principal. He addressed each student as "Mr." and, of course, we were expected to address him as "Dr. DeHuff" and all our teachers as "Mr." There were few women teachers at Poly at that time—Miss Calvert, who taught French, being the only one that I recall. Although there was no formal dress code in the school, Dr. DeHuff's mantra as he roamed the halls of Poly and greeted students was "Remember, all good Poly boys wear ties." And wear ties we did, for fear of being called out by Dr. DeHuff.

Unlike all the other public high schools in the city where a grade of 60 was considered a passing grade, at Poly you had to get a 70 to pass a course. And at Poly, all the courses were considered major courses and therefore all of them—even the so-called non-academic shop courses—entered into calculating a student's grade point average. My manual dexterity being what it was, I came close to not passing the several shop courses I, along with all the other Poly students, were required to take, classes such as patternmaking (designing and making the wooden patterns that metal sand castings are made from) and mechanical drawing (the detailed and highly structured drawing of plans and blueprints). The just-passing grade of 70 I received in both patternmaking and mechanical drawing notwithstanding—I managed to hammer out a grade of 80 in Mr. Freedman's forge and foundry courses—I did well enough in my academic courses to end my 10th-grade at Poly with a grade-point average of 87.

The academic highlight of my time at Poly was getting a grade of 100 in my Plane Geometry final exam. I wasn't so amazed to receive that grade—all it seemed to require was memorization of theorems then logically fitting them together—

but my brother Charlie couldn't get over it. As he had a great interest in mathematics—and later went on to receive a Masters degree in that field—he was prouder than I was of my perfect score in that exam. To me, it was simply a matter of memorizing the theorems, something I found fairly easy to do, and then applying them. I didn't see why he made such a big fuss about it, but he did.

The extra-curricular highlights of my time at Poly were twofold. Following in Charlie's footsteps, I went out for the cheerleading squad and made it. Although hardly physically imposing, and not what one would call a leader at that age, I nevertheless enjoyed leading cheers at the football games Poly played. Then there was the *Poly Follies*. Every year, Poly put on a show to raise money for extracurricular activities. Because it was an all-boys high school, the boys played the roles of any females in the cast—dressed in gender-appropriate costumes, of course—a source of much merriment to the audiences. My brothers before me had participated in that annual tradition at the school, so naturally I did, too, wearing a skirt and a wig as part of the chorus line in the extravaganza in which I participated. It was *The Girl of the Golden West,* a show adapted from a musical Western film of the same name that came out some 15 years earlier.

After just one year at Poly, I was blindsided again: a decision was made to transfer me to another school. My mother feared that I was not making friends or advancing socially at Poly, and she arranged for me to transfer to the other all-boys public high school in Baltimore, Baltimore City College (despite its name, a high school, the oldest in Baltimore and one of the oldest in the country). By that time, owing to the additional year I saved by going to School 49, I was now two-and-a-half years younger than most of the other people in my class. On top of that, I was small for my age and so always the "peewee" of my class. But I didn't care that I was not the social butterfly my mother wanted me to be. I accepted the fact that my age and stature put me at a disadvantage in making friends among my classmates; I had friends in the neighborhood, and I was fine with that.

Mom came to her pronouncement swiftly and with little notice, although when she did broach it to me, I resisted the change, supported in my arguments by Charlie. I did not want to go to City. Not only was it a traditional rival of Poly, but also it was, at the time, not nearly as good a school as Poly. Mom prevailed, though, and I was transferred out of Poly. On my last day there, the Poly counselor handed me the papers necessary to effect my transfer to give to the administrators at City. On top of the stack of forms, where my Poly grade-point average of 87 was reported, he had penned a note to his counterpart at City that read, "If you don't want this boy, I'll gladly take him back."

Through the first half of the 1950's, Baltimore was a segregated city—not as vehemently segregationist as cities farther south, but segregated just the same. Maryland had stayed nominally with the North in the Civil War, but its loyalty was so much in question that Union troops placed cannons on Baltimore's Federal Hill aimed at City Hall lest Mobtown live up to its nickname. The schools, amusement parks, swimming pools, hotels, movie houses, restaurants, mental hospitals, and most other public and commercial facilities were segregated, either by law or by custom (although I don't recall that transit vehicles and water fountains were). Poly had an accelerated curriculum its students could elect to take, the so-called A-course, which stood for Advanced College Preparatory Course. Since none of the black high schools had a similar curriculum, a court action was brought by the local chapter of the National Association for the Advancement of Colored People, argued by Baltimore native Thurgood Marshall—who later went on to become the nation's first black Supreme Court justice. On the grounds that the lack of an A-course in all of the all-black high schools made for an unequal, and therefore discriminatory, education for the black population, the NAACP prevailed, and the year after I was transferred out of Poly, it accepted its first black students. Within a few years after that, all Baltimore schools were desegregated—without much trouble—as a result of the landmark *Brown vs. Board of Education* Supreme Court decision that the Baltimore A-course decision undoubtedly prepared the way for.

Baltimore City College, the high school to which I was transferred, had a fierce football rivalry with Poly dating back to 1888, and transferring to City from Poly was considered tantamount to treason (not by my father, though, as he had gone to City a few years after arriving in this country). City, at least then, was not as rigorous a high school as Poly. And, worse, I didn't like its cheerleading style, so I didn't try out for cheerleading there, as I had at Poly. I did join the Radio Broadcasting Club and the Drama Club, though. In one of the productions the Drama Club put on, I called upon my drama experience as a "girl" in the *Poly Follies* to play a Mammy Yokum back country type in a play we put on. My opening line, spoken as I looked resignedly into the distance: "Thar he goes Ollie. Thar goes your Paw with that durn hound dog Jake."

Baltimore City College was located in a fairly new building in the style of a Gothic castle perched on top of a hill, giving it a commanding view of north Baltimore. Unlike Poly, whose square-block "campus" consisted of unrelenting concrete, City sat atop its hill amid an oasis of green. Its alumni even took to calling the school "The Castle on the Hill." Boys who cut classes would often spend time wandering around the spacious grassy campus until they decided to go back in. One day, I decided to follow their lead, if only to find out more about this practice that was common among City's students. I wandered aimlessly around the school's extensive grounds on my class-cutting adventure that day but didn't see the attraction of it, and I never did it again.

The academic highlight of my time at City was the term paper I submitted for Mr. Cherubin's English class on the Hat-field-McCoy feud. As I did with most term paper assignments in high school—and subsequently in college—I spent the semester feverishly researching the topic and taking notes on index cards, and then, only the night before the paper was due, feverishly organizing the notes and writing the paper itself in my cramped, almost illegible scrawl. I received a good grade on the term paper from Mr. Cherubin, but more meaningful to me than that was the fascination I found in the deep enmities and the motivations for those enmities between the two families that were the subject of the paper. Another area in a similar realm I found absorbing during my high school years was polar exploration. I read everything I could on that subject of extreme fascination for me and often chose it as a topic for themes I had to write.

—————

I graduated from high school in 1954. That fall, at the age of 15, I entered The Johns Hopkins University in Baltimore. I had applied for admission solely to Hopkins, as my attending that university was foreordained by three factors: expectation, affordability, and survivability. My parents' expectations were that all their children would live at home until they married—that's just the way it was in my family and many other first-generation families that we knew. Both Leonard and Bill had gone to Hopkins for their undergraduate studies and commuted from home. Hopkins's undergraduate school at that time being for males only, it would not admit Margie even if she had applied, so she went to then all-female Goucher College in suburban Towson, Maryland, also commuting from home. Charlie went to the University of Maryland College of Pharmacy in downtown Baltimore. In that way, the children in the family fulfilled my parents' expectations of living at home through college and then afterward until they were married.

As for affordability, although my high school grades were good, they weren't good enough to qualify me at many places for full financial aid covering both tuition *and* room and board. That was brought home to me when I attended a college recruiting evening at a classmate's house toward the end of my junior year in high school. The recruiter, who had traveled to Baltimore from Franklin and Marshall College in Lancaster, Pennsylvania, told me at the end of our interview, "Frankly, son, you can't afford to pay both tuition and living expenses at Franklin and Marshall. You're better off applying to someplace local." Since my family could not afford anyplace where I had to pay both tuition and room and board, my choice was, perforce, limited to colleges in Baltimore. And since the best undergraduate institution in Baltimore was The Johns Hopkins University, that's the only one to which I applied. The calculus was simple: Get a job each summer to earn as much as I could of Hopkins's $800 annual tuition, and live at home as before to obviate the need to pay college room and board expenses.

In addition, I hoped that going to Johns Hopkins in Baltimore would not be such a large leap into the unknown for me, a green 15-year-old. I reasoned that my environment would be similar to what I had been experiencing all along: I wouldn't be leaving home and moving to another city, I could even take some of the same public transit buses to Hopkins as I took to get to my high school, I would be in another all-male educational environment, and I would have some of my high school classmates around me in this new environment—other "locals" who also had been accepted to Hopkins. And even I suspected, in my heart of hearts, that, entering college at so tender an age, I did not have the social or life skills to survive very well in such an environment completely on my own.

Being two to three years younger than most of the students in my entering class, I had the distinct feeling that my fellow students were more savvy and worldly-wise than I. Too, many were guys who came from places other than Baltimore and had seen more of the world than I had. I believed I just did not have the life experience to make decisions and act as confidently upon them as they could. And, in fact, upon entering Hopkins, I indeed felt a bit like an outsider naïf in a world of knowing older boys.

A couple of potent examples early in my college career illustrate my lack of worldly-wisdom and mature social graces. On the first day of classes at Hopkins, I came late to Dr. Sidney Painter's Introduction to Western Civilization class. Wearing ersatz "tough guy" shoes that had steel taps on both the heels and the soles, I entered the lecture hall, and—my shoes clacking loudly—I blithely took the steps up the center aisle of the small amphitheater to find a seat. The stately Dr. Painter stopped his lecture to stare coldly at this tardy interloper, and everyone else in the classroom fell utterly silent as I tap-tap-tapped my way to an empty seat at the top of the lecture hall. Once I was seated and the echo of my tap shoes dissipated, Dr. Painter shook his head in disdain and resumed his lecture.

In the first weeks of the semester, the fraternities on campus held "rush parties" to which incoming freshmen were invited in order to look over and evaluate the fraternity members, and vice versa. The first rush party I went to was given by Phi Sigma Delta, of which my brother, Bill, had been a member. On entering the fraternity house, a beer was thrust into my hand. Being not only young but also slight for my age, I got so intoxicated so fast on that one beer that all I remember of the evening was finding myself sitting on the stairs leading down to the fraternity house basement mumbling incoherently. I was not "tapped" for Phi Sigma Delta.

Although I was "tapped" for Alpha Epsilon Pi, I did not pledge any fraternity in my freshman year, deciding, uncharac-teristically wisely, to take a year to think about it as I tried to figure out this whole college thing. I joined AEPi in my sopho-more year, but after experiencing fraternity life for that year, I became less and less active as a member. I did not have the filial feeling toward my fraternity "brothers" I was supposed to have, so why should they be my friends if the only thing we had in common was that we joined the same fraternity? Perhaps if I had lived at the fraternity house as some of my fraternity brothers did, sharing more of our lives together, I would have felt differently.

It was not all that uncommon then to be a live-at-home commuter while a Hopkins student, although the situation currently on that campus, more than 50 years later, is very different. Now, almost all entering freshmen live on campus, but when I entered in 1954, of the 380 boys in my entering class, I estimate that roughly 40 percent were from the greater Baltimore area, with only a minority of those locals opting as freshmen to live on campus or in a fraternity house. Being a daily commuter put one at a disadvantage, however, for the social and intellectual life on campus revolved around the campus residents. Because I was too young during my freshman year to have a driver's license—and even after I turned 16 and obtained a license but did not have a car of my own—every day I would have to take three city transit buses to reach the Hopkins campus halfway across town at the edge of Baltimore's Roland Park neighborhood. With the journey between home and campus amounting to almost an hour each way, I remained at school on the days when I didn't have back-to-back classes, studying in the library and returning home late in the afternoon to have supper and then hitting the books some more. After almost a year of commuting this way, I did arrange to get rides some days with classmates who lived near me, had access to a car, and had schedules that approximated mine.

In the year before entering college, I had thought long and hard about what I might major in. My oldest brothers, Len and Bill, were engineering majors at Hopkins, but I knew right off that I didn't have the interest or aptitude to pursue that line of work. I thought briefly about dentistry until someone pointed out that I would need a good bit of manual dexterity for that, which I didn't think I had. Plus, it dawned on me that, as a dentist, I would be placing my hands in other people's mouths a good deal of the time, a thought that didn't appeal to me. I did like trying to place myself in other people's minds, though, so I elected to major in psychology, which put me in another minority at Hopkins. Roughly one-third of the undergraduate student body there were pre-medical students, another one-third were science and engineering majors, and the remaining one-third majored in one of the many remaining fields.

Being among a small cadre of psychology majors, of which there were probably no more than 20 in the whole undergraduate student body of 1,200 at the time, did have its advantages, though. The year—my sophomore year—I formally declared psychology as my major, the psychology department moved into a brand new, spacious building on the Hopkins campus, Ames Hall. Once any of our small cadre of undergraduate majors had advanced far enough to conduct our own research, we were given offices in Ames Hall in which to work—something few other undergraduates could enjoy. There, at night, we undergraduate psychology majors (among them Roger McKinley, Jay Harris, Lenny Horowitz, and Al Marston) could interact informally with one another as well as even—an almost unheard of privilege—with the graduate students.

Sharing offices in the same building with the rest of the department led to a feeling of closeness with the faculty, as well. I have fond memories of often being around, talking with, and absorbing knowledge from Mary Ainsworth, James Deese, and Wendell Garner, among other faculty members of the department. Jim Deese was an earnest experimental psychologist whose courses in experimental psychology I took to with great enthusiasm and who was also my academic advisor. As part of his course on learning, I spent hours with rats in the lab minutely and obsessively recording manually their every press of the Skinner box bar to receive food reinforcement. I wasn't uncovering any new knowledge through this, but I was discovering for myself how these organisms learned and how psychologists learned to learn how they learned. I had even greater interest in the subjects of personality and developmental psychology and took many courses with the only psychology department faculty member who taught such courses, Mary Ainsworth.

Wendell ("Tex") Garner taught statistics—never one of my favorite subjects and one I learned to master only with effort. My warmest memory of him goes back not to the classroom but to an incident outside of the classroom. Snow unexpectedly began to fall mid-morning one day and continued the rest of the day. By the time I left campus late that afternoon to catch the first of my three buses home, traffic was considerably clogged because Baltimore did not handle snowstorms well. After waiting for my first bus for more than half an hour, I sensed that it was not going to reach my stop just outside of campus during the storm. I decided to walk the two miles to Cold Spring Lane in the hope that I could at least catch the second bus I had to take to get home.

As I slogged my way bootless through the snow along University Parkway, a car stopped ahead of me. As I approached it, I saw that it was driven by the department head, Dr. Garner. He rolled his car window down and asked, "Where are you walking to in this weather?" When I told him of my plight, he offered me a ride, which I gladly took, to my next bus route on Cold Spring Lane. A mere undergraduate, I did not expect to be noticed, much less helped, by the head of the psychology department. As luck would have it, that bus and the one after it made it through the storm, so I arrived home safely—if also cold, wet, and late. Dr. Garner's kind act deprived me of the ability to tell my grandchildren the clichéd story of having to "walk miles in the snow to get to and from school," but I was gratified that the closeness we all felt as members of a small department facilitated kind acts like his.

Although I earned good grades throughout high school, I did not readily duplicate that accomplishment at Hopkins. Known as a "cut-throat" school where the undergraduates competed for good grades on the ubiquitous grading curve—and in a learning environment dominated by pre-med and engineering students who fought hard and competitively for the relatively few high grades on that curve—it was not as easy for me to earn the kind of grades I did in high school. I received C's in every one of my non-psychology courses, with one exception— a barely passing D in physics one semester. But I earned straight A's or better in all my psychology courses. How, you might ask, could I earn a grade better than A in a college course? Hopkins students who did exceptionally well in a course (with the accent on "exceptionally") could be given, at the professor's discretion, a grade of H, which stood for Honors. In every one of the several courses I took with Dr. Ainsworth in the fields I was especially interested in—developmental and personality psychology—I earned an H. Good thing, too, as the H's and A's I received in my psychology courses served to counterbalance the C's I earned in my other courses when it came to calculating my overall grade point average.

Even though I was a commuter at Johns Hopkins, I became close friends with two dorm residents who were in my year. Both were New Yorkers, both lived in the dormitories on campus and were friends with each other, and both were pre-med majors. Irwin and Neal were great guys, and I spent a lot of interesting time with them even though I was a local, not a dorm resident like they were. I spent so much time with them that I unconsciously lost my Baltimore accent—which I had grown to find extremely grating on the ear anyway—substituting, also unconsciously, their New York accent in its place.

The Johns Hopkins University had a strict academic honor code to which I adhered conscientiously, as did all of the other students, as far as I could tell. Cheating on exams, copying others' homework assignments, and similar transgressions were not tolerated and were to be reported immediately to an Honor Commission composed entirely of fellow Hopkins undergraduates. One day before heading off to his home in New York for the annual Christmas break, Irwin asked—since I was local and therefore remaining in town over the break—if I would retrieve a package he was expecting in the mail. He was very concerned that it reach his campus mailbox and similarly concerned that it remain safe until he could retrieve it upon his return to campus after the holiday. He instructed me to check his student mailbox in the on-campus post office periodically over the vacation period and to hold this valuable package for him. I agreed and diligently followed his instructions, which included opening the package once it arrived to confirm that it was what he was waiting for and reporting this to him by telephone.

When the package arrived, I duly opened it and gave its contents a cursory glance, as Irwin had asked me to do, then called him in New York to let him know that the package he was expecting had arrived. When I looked a little further at it after the call, however, I got a severe jolt. The package contained a term-paper-like report on a biology subject prepared specifically for Irwin that looked to me as if it could possibly be something he could turn in as his own work. I never felt the prick of the horns of a dilemma as sharply and painfully as this one. There could be a perfectly innocent explanation for it, I thought, and, moreover, I doubted that Irwin—an extremely bright person—would be so dumb as to expose a fellow student to a scheme in which he was aiming to turn in a paper as his own without having done the required work. On the other hand, it looked to me that the paper he ordered could very well be a component of a cheating scheme. The honor code required immediate reporting of any suspected transgressions, yet the situation could easily have had an entirely innocent explanation. My reporting of it could subject both Irwin and me to embarrassment and rebuke, in addition to causing him potentially not to graduate or be admitted to medical school if he were found guilty of violating the honor code.

After a couple days of worrying over the issue almost every waking minute—keeping it all inside me—I decided I had no other choice but to report the situation to the Honor Commission to decide upon it. Once classes resumed, the Honor Commission held an honor code trial at which I had to testify, as did Irwin. I was not privy to either Irwin's testimony or the commission's deliberations, but I was told by an Honor Commission member after the hearing that it had not found him to be in violation of the honor code. I was glad that he had been found not to be in violation, and equally glad that I had adhered to what I thought was the right thing to do. But my doing so cost me my friendship with my friends from New York and, in turn, any further immersion I might have had in the life of those who lived on campus. Irwin and Neal never gave me the time of day after that. Irwin went on after graduation to one of the country's top medical schools and became a prominent physician.

When May of 1958 came around, I looked forward to graduating from Hopkins along with the roughly 300 or so of my classmates who had made it all the way through our four years together. Some people can boast that the President of the United States was the speaker at their college commencement. My classmates and I can boast that the President of the United States merely *introduced* the main speaker at our graduation ceremony. This came about because the president of The Johns Hopkins University, Dr. Milton Eisenhower, used his brotherly connections to request that U.S. President Dwight D. Eisenhower attend the graduation ceremony. Harold Macmillan, then Prime Minister of the United Kingdom, was scheduled to be on an official state visit to Washington at the time of the commencement, and it was arranged for him to be the commencement speaker. Thus it was that President Dwight Eisenhower and Prime Minister Harold Macmillan helicoptered over to the Hopkins Homewood campus from Washington, D.C. on graduation day. And thus it was that University president Milton Eisenhower played third banana by introducing to the audience United States President Dwight David Eisenhower, who in turn played second banana to Prime Minister of the

United Kingdom Harold Macmillan by introducing him as the commencement speaker.

The year before graduation, I started thinking about what I would do once I graduated from Hopkins. Almost anything in the fields of psychology that interested me—personality and child development, perceptual development, clinical psychology—required a doctoral degree to pursue it meaningfully. In addition, I liked the life of the mind that I saw modeled before me by the faculty and graduate students at Johns Hopkins. I explored graduate study options with my adviser, Dr. Deese, who was a hard-headed experimental psychologist, the farthest thing, conceptually, from a "soft-headed" clinical psychologist (although I was to find out later that he was married to one). He advised me, wisely, that, given my academic strengths and broad interests, I should search out graduate programs that would allow me to spread my wings, intellectually and research-wise, beyond those immediate fields of interest.

I followed his advice and decided to apply to graduate programs in clinical psychology, but programs that encouraged students to explore and do research in other psychological disciplines. My thinking was that if I could not make a living as a research psychologist, I could always fall back on working as a clinical psychologist, as the world had an unending need for professionals who could help people sort out their problems.

Many graduate programs in clinical psychology in that era offered full rides, financially, consisting of both tuition and a stipend for living expenses. I envisioned that I would be able to swing it on my own under those conditions, and so I spent the summer before, and the early part of, my senior year exploring the available graduate programs in clinical psychology, their orientations, and the financial support they might provide.

But I had to negotiate another hurdle before I applied to

any of them. Aunt Helen, my mother's older sister, had gotten wind of my plans for graduate school and came to our house for a serious discussion with my mother (whom she called "Fan") and me. Helen was a powerful and domineering force of nature who could easily intimidate anyone—including my mother—to whom she addressed her well-chosen words. "After studying all those years, what kind of living is he going to make, Fan, as a clinical psychologist?" she asked my mother.

I knew from my investigations that I could make a living, if not a lavish one, but both Mom and Aunt Helen had little conception of what those possibilities were, much less what a clinical psychologist did. Almost the only professional fields Jewish mothers of their era could conceive of for their children were physician, lawyer, teacher, pharmacist, dentist, engineer, or accountant. "You should go to graduate school to become a petroleum engineer," Aunt Helen pronounced with all the confident, overbearing force of the well-practiced and highly successful attorney she was. She continued her argument, concluding with the coup de grace: "That's the coming thing, you know: Petroleum engineers and petrogeologists make lots of money working for oil companies."

A petroleum engineer? There's nothing wrong with being one, but being woefully ill-equipped to be an engineer of any type, having little interest in choosing my ultimate vocation on the premise it would make me lots of money, and having no interest at all in exploring for oil, I had already decided what I wanted to do with the rest of my life. I mumbled something to that effect, but they kept the pressure on.

Once this little family conclave thankfully ended—save for an occasional back-and-forth with Mom or Aunt Helen about it—I put it out of my mind for the unrealistic notion it was. By that point in my life I had started to move away from allowing my mother, much less her older sister, to make important decisions for me. I now understand the underlying concern this issue represented to them. They had to scrimp and save to get to, and then through, law school and achieve whatever level of economic comfort and security they reached. They firmly believed that "nice Jewish children" should enter professions that would provide prestige and economic security. It did not even occur to them that my decisions about my future would include other considerations that I might think were important.

That summer, I chose eight schools offering graduate study in clinical psychology to apply to, ranging from "impossible dream" ones at major universities from which I thought my overall grades at Hopkins would be unlikely to elicit an offer of admission (Harvard, Yale, Illinois, Indiana, and Michigan) to three that had interesting programs to which I thought I would have a better chance of gaining admission (Washington University of St. Louis, Clark University, and The University of Rochester).

I was particularly excited by the prospect of going to one of the latter two schools, as they both had programs where clinical psychology was not walled off from the rest of the psychology department as it was in many other places. In fact, graduate students in clinical in those two programs were encouraged to learn about, and conduct research in, the other subdisciplines of psychology. In March of my senior year, I traveled to the annual conference of the Eastern Psychological Association in New York to talk with a faculty member in each of these programs—Dr. Morton Wiener of Clark (who had earned his doctorate at The University of Rochester) and Dr. Emory Cowen of Rochester—to obtain first-hand information on both those programs to which I had applied.

All graduate programs in psychology agreed not to inform applicants of their admission decisions prior to April 1st, and in turn, all applicants had until April 15th to inform the programs whether or not they would accept their offers of admission. On April 1st of my senior year I received the highly anticipated eight letters. I opened them in a lather of expectancy to find I was accepted to four of the programs: Indiana University, Washington University, Clark University, and The University of Rochester. Indiana offered me tuition and a teaching assistantship, but I decided not to accept their offer of admission because I realized their program was a more quantitatively oriented one than I really wanted. Washington University offered me no financial support, so I quickly informed them that I could not attend under those conditions. They wrote back a short time afterward to tell me that they could offer me financial support after all, but by that time, my decision process was too far along to change my mind about entering their program.

That left Clark University and The University of Rochester—both of which offered me full tuition and a fellowship stipend for living expenses—for me to inform, by April 15th, of my decision. The next two weeks were agonizing. I thought both programs were just the kind of programs I would like, both offered full financial support, and I believed I would be happy in either of them. That did not help my decision-making at all. By the morning of April 15th, my agonizing still had not brought me to a definite decision on where to spend the next four years of my life. I could intellectualize it no further, though. I had to make a decision and trust my gut, and my gut told me to choose The University of Rochester. It was a decision I did not regret later in life, but I was comforted by the feeling that had I chosen Clark University, from what I knew about it then and have learned since, I would not have regretted attending that university for my graduate studies, either.

My parents were not happy that I was planning to leave home to attend graduate school 400 miles away. All my brothers, as well as my sister, had lived at home until they were married. How, and why, could I do this? my parents asked me, as if I were being naïve at best and traitorous at worst. And this for an eventual profession and career they did not fully understand and which they worried would not provide a secure future for me. But I was determined to move onward, and I spent the summer months after my graduation from Hopkins preparing both mentally and physically for the new journey on which I was determined to embark.

After I left for graduate school, my parents kept my bedroom intact in the hope that I would eventually return to it and live with them until I was married, as my siblings all had done. It was a vain hope, but I can't fault them for thinking that way—it was no different from the way most parents of their generation with similar backgrounds thought.

I had graduated college and was starting graduate study at the age of 19. Looking back across the years, do I appreciate having had the capability to finish my education up to that point two to three years before most of my peers? I think I would have been bored throughout my elementary and secondary education had I not been advanced in grades. The voluminous research coming from The Study of Mathematically Precocious Youth, the longest-running longitudinal study of intellectually talented children as they grow up, has indicated that those who had been given special accommodations, like skipping grades and taking advanced studies in junior and senior high school, achieve much more than their equally smart peers who were not given those special accommodations. I certainly have appreciated the fact that I got a jump on starting my career after graduate school while I was so young and consequently was able to retire a few years earlier than the usual age of retirement.

On the other hand, having been skipped a half-grade here and a half-grade there during my schooling, I did miss out on certain areas of knowledge. And I did not have the maturity when I entered college to fully partake of the college experience. All things considered, though, I'm glad to have done it the way I did.

7

IN MY SPARE TIME

"Life is more fun if you play games."
— Roald Dahl, *My Uncle Oswald*

I REMEMBER THE OLD neighborhood especially for the gang of kids in it and the games we played. Until my teen years, my regular neighborhood group of playmates consisted of Leonard Adler, Howard Bernstein, Arnie Berkenfeld, Paul Greenfeld, Norman Kronberg, Walter 'Buddy' Miller, Howard 'Butch' Rothschild, and several other boys. As preteens, we didn't hang around, or play, with girls. On afternoons when we didn't have Hebrew School after regular school, and certainly on weekend days when we had no school at all, the neighborhood boys congregated on Westbury Avenue on the block that ran between Holmes Avenue and Woodbrook Avenue, to play. Sometimes we would just hang out and talk, talk that occasionally ended in scuffles with one another. I tried to avoid serious scuffles, for I didn't like pain (imagine that). One time, though, Buddy Miller and I got into a fight. For five minutes, we grappled and grabbed at each other, trying to inflict pain with our grabs and twists. I hated it. After watching this epic battle for a while, the other kids saved me from more unpleasantness by breaking us up, and Buddy and I retreated to our "neutral corners."

Most times, though, our afternoons consisted of playing street games. Our daytime games included Red Light, Three Steps to Germany, boxball, stickball, stepball, territory, marbles, wallball, areyball, wireball, kick the can, and hide-and-go-seek.

In Red Light, the person who was "it" stood by the curb facing the rest of the kids spread out in a line on the other side of the street. "It" would turn his back, which gave the signal for the other kids to start advancing in single steps toward him. "It" counted rapidly to ten, and then shouted "1-2-3 Red Light!", at which point the advancing line was supposed to stop. If, after turning back around, "It" spotted one of the others still moving, the offender had to return to the starting line. The whole routine was repeated until someone reached "It," where-upon that person became "It." Three Steps to Germany was basically a war-era variation of Red Light; when World War II ended, that game went out of style.

Our version of boxball—a game peculiar to Baltimore, I would guess—was a form of baseball, but without the bat, the hardball, or gloves. We chalked a diamond about fifteen feet on a side on the Westbury Avenue asphalt, drawing bases at all four corners and a pitcher's box in the center. The pitcher tossed a tennis ball, underhand, toward the hitter at home plate, the rule being that the ball had to bounce once before reaching the hitter. The hitter used his open hand to hit the ball, and, if he did, he ran the bases while the players on the opposing team ran to get the ball to try to tag him out. The Davidoffs had a house on the corner of Westbury and Holmes Avenues with a small side yard surrounded by hedges of which Mrs. Davidoff was very protective. Woe betide the player who hit the ball into the Davidoffs' yard. When that occurred, it became a race to retrieve the ball from her yard—by jumping the hedges that bordered it— before Mrs. Davidoff could run out of her house and get it, yelling all the while at "You damned kids with your

damned balls." If she got there before one of us did, she kept
the ball, and it was lost to us forever.

Our version of stickball was also probably peculiar to Baltimore—or, for all I know, just our neighborhood. We played it
in the narrow alley that ran behind Holmes Avenue and Auchentroly Terrace, with a minimum of two boys per team. One end
of the alley dead-ended at a high concrete retaining wall that
served as a perfect backstop for the pitches, and, consequently,
no catcher was needed. Virtually no equipment was needed,
either; just a sawed-off broomstick for a bat and a tennis ball
for a ball. Being played in a narrow alleyway, there wasn't
room to set up bases and do base running, so hits were determined by the distance the ball was hit—three backyard lengths
was a single, four was a double, five, a triple, and six, a home
run. Of course, if the ball was caught by either the pitcher or
the opposing team's fielder, the batter was out.

I believe our versions of kick the can and hide-and-go-seek
were the same as played elsewhere, so I won't bore you with
details of those games.

Even if there were not enough boys around to play group
games, there were always two-player games to play. One of
these was stepball. The player who was up would throw a tennis
ball against the concrete steps of whatever house we were
playing at, and it would be deemed an out, single, double, triple,
or home run depending on whether the opposing player caught
it on the fly or where it bounced before he got to it. Another
two-person game we played was called territory. We'd find a
bare patch of ground (easy enough to find in my neighborhood)
and, using a pocket knife, scratch a rectangular box into it, with
another line bisecting it in the middle, creating two "territories."
Each of the two players would flip the knife in turn into the
ground within the confines of the other player's territory. If it
did not stick in the ground, he lost his turn to the other player.
If it did stick in the ground, the thrower drew a line in the direction the edge of the blade was pointing until it reached one of

that territory's borders. If that line reached the border between the two territories, the player could erase the boundary line and continue with his knife point, enlarging his own territory. Each player's territory would be made smaller or larger by successive knife throws until one player's territory dominated, or, as more usually happened, the two players tired of the game and called it quits.

Another two-player game we played on a bare patch of ground on Westbury Avenue was marbles. Beyond the "standard" version of marbles, a variation we played centered around a hole dug into the dirt with one's heel. Each player tossed or shot a marble attempting to get it into the hole. Once his marble got into the hole, he could remove it from the hole and place it one foot length away in any direction, then shoot it from there trying to hit any loose marbles of the opposing player that didn't make it to the hole. The shooting player then got to keep whatever marbles he hit.

We played wallball on the high wall of one of the Woodbrook Avenue apartment buildings that sided onto Westbury Avenue. That game consisted of one player throwing a tennis ball against the wall above a fixed height and the opposing player trying to catch it as it came down. Sometimes we played it against two opposing walls in the narrow area-way—or "areyway," as we called it—between two of the apartment buildings, throwing the ball against one wall hard enough for it to ricochet against the opposite wall. That game was played in the "areyway," so that's why we called it areyball. Our third variation on the theme of wallball, wireball, was played in the area-way between two of the buildings where, about twelve feet up on one of the buildings, three parallel electric wires ran horizontally, offset from the building wall by glass electric insulators. In this variation of wallball, the thrower threw the ball against one wall trying to get the ball to reach the offset wires on the opposite wall to become entangled in them. Successful entangling made it much harder for the opposing player to catch the ball as it came down.

Whenever 4:30 in the afternoon came, our afternoon games broke up as if by a magic invisible signal beckoning us from the radio. It was time for everyone to head home to listen to the radio serials broadcast every weekday starting at 4:45. At one time or another, these 15-minute radio programs featured the likes of Dick Tracy, Captain Marvel, Hop Harrigan, Tom Mix, Red Ryder, Gene Autry, Jack Armstrong—the All-American Boy, Terry and the Pirates, Sky King, and similar western and adventure heroes. Many of these radio programs were sponsored by cereal companies that touted they would send you—if you sent in the required number of boxtops—a "magnificent," "amazing," "rare," or "exciting" prize, "sure to make you the envy of every kid on the block." Who could resist that? The one I remember bursting with anticipation most to see arrive in our mailbox was the Lone Ranger atomic bomb ring, offered by Kix cereal for one boxtop and 15 cents. Daily for two weeks I rushed to see if it had come in the day's mail. This amazing ring, which was offered within a year after the first atomic bomb exploded over Hiroshima, Japan, featured a bomb-shaped object mounted on an adjustable ring. When one end of the bomb ornament was taken off—enabling that hollow end to be used as a secret message compartment, of course—light struck an exposed lens inside the "bomb" causing scintillations to dance across the lens covering the "atom chamber." I could actually watch an atomic reaction—or so I was led to believe! It endlessly fascinated me, this true miracle of modern atomic science.

On April 12, 1945, when the Tom Mix show normally aired at 5:30 in the afternoon, Tom was not there. Instead, sad, elegiac music was playing as an announcer came on to say, in a grave and somber tone, that President Roosevelt had died just a few hours before. I was shocked beyond knowing what to do. President Roosevelt was the only president I had known my whole life. He was *my* president, just as my mother and my father were *my* mother and *my* father. I couldn't imagine life without this President. He was always there during the war, assuring us that we would prevail, and now, with the war within sight of being won, he was gone. I cried on hearing the news, fearful now of the future. My family did their best to comfort me in the face of their obvious sadness, too. President Roosevelt had led the nation to almost the end of World War II, and we all now wondered what we would do without him. My father went down to Pennsylvania Station to see the train that carried FDR's body as it passed through from Washington to its final resting place in Hyde Park, New York. For days afterward a pall hung in the air as our family and the nation as a whole strove to carry on with a new, virtually unknown President, Harry S Truman, leading a dangerous war on two fronts to its conclusion.

Most Saturdays represented a change from the after-school playing we did during the week. On Saturdays, kids in the neighborhood went to the Linden Theater or the Rialto Theater, both within sight of one another on North and Linden Avenues, for a day of movies. That's when 300 screaming nine-, ten-, and eleven-year-olds would pour into each of these movie houses to watch its Saturday matinee marathon of a double feature—a Western and an action/adventure movie—a cliff-

hanging serial like *Flash Gordon*, multiple cartoons, a newsreel, and previews of coming attractions, all for 12 cents. Add the five cents it cost for candy—for me, always a Goldenberg's Peanut Chew—and the five cents it cost for the streetcar ride each way, and for a little over a quarter parents would be rid of their antsy children for a good part of each Saturday.

When the school year ended, we had even more recreational options. With no school and no homework, we had the daylight hours all to our own. A memorable summertime adventure I had one time with my friends took place at a swale in Druid Hill Park, just across busy Auchentroly Terrace from Shaarei Tfiloh synagogue. One of the kids in the neighborhood discovered that a huge tree had fallen the night before during a thunderstorm, so we decided to take a look at it. When we got there, we encountered a situation that had adventure written all over it. The tree had fallen across the swale, its roots and trunk on one side of it and its crown on the other. The fallen tree's branches pointed every which way, some down into the swale, others up toward the sky, stimulating the minds of the 10-year-old explorers who came by to play there with great ideas of adventure. Starting after lunch, we played the rest of the day on it, imagining it at times as an airplane, a fort, a hidden forest, a castle. In our state of glee and adventure, none of us noticed the sun setting. When we finally could not see one another, we called it quits and headed for home, tired, dirty, and happy.

When I got home, my parents and brothers were beside themselves with worry. "Where were you all day?" Mom asked. "I sent your brothers out to look for you when you didn't come home for supper, we were so worried." My brothers chimed in with a recitation of the places they went to look for me, but none included the tangled branches of the downed tree. I wasn't punished for my transgression—that wasn't my parents' style—

but Mom told me in very clear terms always to stay aware of the time when I went out to play and to return home in time for supper. "It's alright to go out again to play after dark with the kids if we let you, but never go away for so long without telling us where you're going," Mom finished her lecture.

One summer day, also at age 10, a bunch of neighborhood kids decided to build a street cart out of an orange crate and some wood we found and to equip it with wheels we had cadged from someone's back yard. Our aim was to blast down the two-block-long hill that was Woodbrook Avenue in our racing cart. Using nails we found in an alley, we hammered the orange crate—the cart's "cabin"—onto a long wooden board—its "frame." We then managed to attach under that board a couple of metal rods we had also found as axles for the wheels. We even figured out a way to steer this beast by pivoting the front axle with our feet as we sat in the orange crate. How to stop it had us stumped until I thought of placing a wooden two-by-four stud behind where the driver sat that would rest lightly on the rear wheels. To stop the cart, all the driver had to do was press his elbows down on the two-by-four behind him hard enough to cause enough friction to slow the wheels to a stop. Our racing cart was a success, and we took turns going from the top of Woodbrook Avenue down the hill. We posted spotters on the corners of Westbury and Woodbrook Avenues to wave automobiles to a stop in case one should intrude on our race-course. It turned out, though, that no orange crate driver was brave enough to go farther than the one block to Westbury Avenue. The fast downhill speed it reached by the time it came to Westbury Avenue, combined with the sluggish braking response, was enough to scare all of us out of continuing on to the next block and to the very bottom of Woodbrook Avenue. Amazingly, no one got hurt from our race car driving.

On the same stretch of Woodbrook Avenue on which we raced our orange-crate racer, however, I did get hurt in a more innocuous pursuit—chasing bubbles. One of the neighborhood boys showed up one day with a bottle of bubble solution that had a bubble-blower formed into its top. We played at making bubbles and then chasing them as they wafted down the street. On one of my turns to chase, I got so absorbed in chasing the bubbles floating above my head that I ran straight into a lamp-post that was planted solidly on the sidewalk. The next thing I knew, I came to on the Naugahyde couch in the den of my house with a washcloth full of ice cubes on my forehead and my mother and sister hovering over me, concerned looks darkening their faces. I don't know who moved me the one block from Woodbrook Avenue to my house the next street over, or how. I had a large bump on my forehead from this incident and was told later that I was unconscious for about 20 minutes.

Lying on the sofa while I regained consciousness was the extent of my treatment for that accident. We didn't go in much for visits to physicians if at all avoidable; they cost money. I recall seeing Dr. Applefeld, our "family physician," only once for anything other than childhood immunizations. I had hurt my arm badly during a bout of roughhousing with my friends and went home in pain from it. When the pain lasted for a couple of days, my mother became alarmed that I might have broken it, so she took me to Dr. Applefeld's office, two blocks away on Reisterstown Road, to have him look at it. Seeing how scared I was to be in his office, he didn't immediately do a formal examination of my arm. Rather, he engaged me in playful conversation and then casually asked me to pull on his arm with my injured arm while he provided resistance. He concluded that my arm wasn't broken, but he still suggested to my mother that I might want to wear a cotton sling "to rest my arm" for a few days. With that, we went home.

Most other ailments in our family—and between five children we had most of the common ones—were treated at home. For colds, fevers, flu (we called it "the grippe"), and headaches, my parents prescribed rest. For upset stomachs, the dreaded enema was the treatment of choice—my parents', not ours.

Fortunately, I have a fairly strong stomach, so I did not have to face the dreaded enema often. Of the few times I did, I can attest that it was very uncomfortable, but very effective. Even the more serious childhood illnesses, like measles, mumps, and chicken pox were not treated very differently from minor colds and fevers. Just days, rather than hours, of bed rest. And fluids— lots of fluids.

I had some close calls in my careless youth. One early evening, I joined my brother Charlie on the lower end of Holmes Avenue, where he was hanging out with his teenage friends. As they were joshing and talking on one of the stoops, I walked into the street. Holmes Avenue was a lightly trafficked street, and I didn't give much thought to wandering onto it then. Just as I stepped off the curb that evening, though, a car I had not noticed came down the street. One of Charlie's friends saw what I had done and how perilously close the car was and rushed out into the street, picked me up bodily, and hauled me over to the curb.

Another near-accident was literally a brush with death. It happened when I was coming home after a day of classes at Poly. The trip home involved taking the streetcar that stopped on North Avenue in front of Poly and then, when it reached North and Linden Avenues, transferring to another one. As I alighted at Linden Avenue, I saw the trolley I intended to transfer to coming up Linden Avenue, and I crossed in front of the streetcar I had just left to catch it. I was so focused visually on the trolley I was trying to catch that my auditory attention was virtually nil, so I was completely oblivious to the sound of a wailing siren on North Avenue. As I crossed in front of the streetcar I had just left, an ambulance sped past on the wrong side of the street. It brushed my jacket with its door handle, tearing it open, but it kept moving on. Reacting to what had just happened, my bladder let go and I wet my pants. Several adults who had seen the incident walked me to the sidewalk at the corner of the street to make sure I was okay and was able to go on my way. Twelve-year-old me was so embarrassed by the wet stain on my pants, I was more concerned with hiding it from the adults who were trying to help me than I was with talking to them. Eventually, I calmed down, dried up, and caught a street car for home. Once home, I told no one what had happened.

Undaunted by any of these perils to life and limb, I decided to enter Baltimore's annual Soap Box Derby. That entailed first building a soap box racer conforming to the specifications provided by *The Baltimore Sun*, the event's sponsor. My father helped me as best he could to saw the wooden chassis base out of a long, thick, wide board; chisel out a depression in it for my bottom to rest in; and so on, all using hand tools, the only kind we had around the house. My father was not handy when it came to home repairs and carpentry. In fact, most of his attempts to make such repairs were half-humorously (but half-seriously) mocked by calling them *khop-lop*, a term that may have been invented by our family. Building the soap box racer entailed a lot of work and took much more know-how than either Dad or I possessed. Before the wooden chassis was done, I saw how much more effort it would take to complete the racer and abandoned the project.

Because it got dark later, a great thing about summer was that we could return to the streets after supper to play more games, some of which stretched into nightfall. Besides hide-and-go-seek (that's what we called it—the name hide-and-seek, without the "go," still sounds strange to my ears), one of our most popular evening games was Red Line, an entirely different game from the aforementioned Red Light. For this game, we scratched the outline of a rectangular box onto the asphalt of Westbury Avenue with a stone. Whoever was "It" had to stand in the box, cover his eyes, and count to 100 while the other participants scattered throughout the neighborhood to hide. "It" then had to leave the box and find each of them, and when he did, grab the person and hold him long enough to say "one-two-three Red Line." Naturally, the would-be captive tried to squirm out of "It's" grasp, often starting a small struggle. But if whoever was "It" held on long enough to utter "one-two-three Red Line," the captive was taken to the box and had to stay imprisoned there. The captive(s) could be freed, though, if another player managed to sneak up to the box when "It" was not around or was otherwise distracted and yell "one-two-three Red Line!" at which point all who were imprisoned in the box were free to run away and hide again. The player designated "It" seldom managed to capture all the opposing players before everyone got exhausted and quit for the night.

But wait, there's more. While other cities and other neighborhoods most likely played Red Line, our neighborhood had a unique variation of it called "Deh-Deh-Deh-Deh." Think of the opening four notes of Beethoven's Fifth Symphony and you've got the right way to sing/say it. In our variation, the boys who ran and hid from the "It" boy were obligated to taunt him from their hiding places—usually in yards or behind garbage cans off the alley, or on the roofs of the garages facing the alley—by singing "deh-deh-deh-deh." This gave "It" a fighting chance to locate his prey, and when he did, he, in turn, was obligated to sing "deh-deh-deh-deh." On those nights we played it, the neighborhood rang out with so many chants of "deh-deh-deh-deh" that the grown-ups must have thought we were rehearsing for a children's chorus of Beethoven's Fifth Symphony.

My gang of kids also engaged in less constructive "games" at night. These consisted of going to Tioga Parkway, another neighborhood on the other side of Brown's estate and literally on the other side of the (streetcar) tracks from us. That neighborhood had larger and nicer lawns in front of the houses that gave it a distinctly more upscale look than ours. Many of those lawns had ropes around them to keep people from walking on the grass. Our gang would take it upon themselves to cut the ropes. While I did not really see how this could be fun, I went along with the other kids so as to remain part of the group, although I hung back from actually cutting the ropes (it made me feel less culpable). The only mischief I did engage in, because I did not feel it was harmful or destructive, was to sneak up on a house from the alley and tape the point end of a pencil to a window. At the other end of the pencil, I had tied a long piece of string. By pulling on the string sporadically, I could cause the pencil to tap the window. In the darkness of the evening, the occupants of the house would be set to wondering what the strange tapping they heard was. If they came out to investigate, I would run away. I never got discovered.

———•—•———

For two weeks each during two summers running, I went to a sleep-away camp. Camp Airy, a boys' camp, was founded earlier in the century by a couple of Baltimore philanthropists as a fresh-air retreat for young Jewish immigrants—and, later, their children. Camp Airy was on a large lake, and a sister camp for girls, Camp Louise, was on the other side of the same lake. The camps offered sessions of two, three, or four weeks, providing young city kids the chance to spend time swimming in the ice-cold lake water and cavorting in fresh mountain air in the summer. The camps were situated 80 miles west of Baltimore in Maryland's Catoctin Mountains, near what is now the presidential retreat, Camp David. The train ride out to Thurmont, Maryland, was an exciting adventure for the young campers from Baltimore, as much of an adventure as the games, races, swimming, and crafts of the camps themselves. By the end of each two-week session I went to, I was a proficient crafter of braided lanyards made of plastic lacing called "gimp," onto which one could attach a whistle. I never figured out any other use for these lanyards, and once home, they found their way to the backs of drawers, where they were ultimately forgotten.

For a couple of other summers, I resolutely planted a vegetable garden in our back yard. "The country" was a place of almost mythical proportions to me, a place where food was created magically by farmers who possessed the special knowledge required to grow the fruits, vegetables, and eggs we bought at the store or from street peddlers. I thought I would try my hand at growing vegetables in order to experience the mystique of the country right there in the city. I told my father of my ambition, and one weekend he and I went to a store to select seeds—radishes, carrots, beans, spring onions—to plant. When the first task came to turn over the scrawny grass in the 5- by 10-foot plot I had envisioned for my back yard garden, reality set in. This was hard work, way harder than I imagined it would be. After seeing me struggle just to open up my hardscrabble patch of nature, Dad came out to help me finish the job. Once we were done, I planted the seeds we had bought and then waited with a 10-year-old's impatience to see what our labors had wrought. I did not neglect to water my garden with a hose from a faucet in the back of the house, but I soon noticed that watering it helped the weeds grow, too. Within a few weeks I had raised a crop of intertwined weeds and scrawny vegetables, and at the end of the summer, few of the latter had grown to a size suitable to place on the table. I tried again the next summer, but with the same results. I left farming—until I was much older—concluding that the soil in the city must just not be as good for growing crops as the soil in the country. There did indeed seem to be something mystical about the country, after all.

———•◦•———

I pursued other hobbies as well. Charlie liked to build model airplanes, and I emulated him in that as I did in so many other things. He showed me how to construct model plane frames by cutting out bulkheads from balsa wood, then stretch balsa wood stringers across the bulkheads and pin and glue them. All this was before the era of much easier plastic models. Once the fuselage, wing, and tail frames were constructed in this manner, we glued thin tissue paper over the whole construction. Then once the glue holding this airplane skin was dry, we wet the paper so that it shrank as it dried and became taut. The final step was to paint the plane's taut skin, first with clear model airplane "dope" (a lacquer-type substance) and then with colored "dope" to achieve a realistic look to the finished model.

We bought our modeling supplies at Goffman's Hobby Shop in downtown Baltimore. I would often go into the shop just to ogle the many wooden model kits they had for sale there—not just planes, but boats, cars, and other speedy vehicles. When I noticed that Goffman's was having a contest to see who could build the best-looking model airplane, I decided to enter. I chose a kit for a P-51 Mustang, a fast propeller-driven fighter plane that played a major role in U.S. air supremacy in World War II. I liked its sleek look, made even sleeker-looking by the underslung air intake at the bottom of its fuselage. I gave the model my best effort, carefully cutting out the parts from balsa wood, gluing them together, and covering them with modeling paper. I painted it silver, just like the real thing, and then painted in the appropriate detail. Once I had brought it in to Goffman's for the contest, I could barely contain myself waiting for the contest results. After a few weeks of nail-biting torture, I heard from them: I had won in my age category! My prize was a medal, inscribed with my name, that was placed in Goffman's window for several weeks, alongside my winning model for all the world to see.

Knowing how proud I was of it, Mom kept the medal in the breakfront in our living room for many years afterward. After she died, my brother Leonard and his wife cleared out my parents' house and sent a box of whatever they found that they thought might be mine up to me in Massachusetts. Alas, the medal was not in the box, and queries I sent to Len and his wife in Baltimore over the distance separating us failed to result in their finding that medal. It's the thing I would have liked most to have had from my parents' house.

———————

As I entered my teen years, my horizons began to widen beyond my friends of younger years and beyond my neighborhood. During those years, three of my buddies and I formed a tight bond, spending weekend days and many summer evenings hitchhiking out of our neighborhood to explore other neighborhoods in the northern half of the city that none of us knew much about. Arnie Berkenfeld and Norman Kronberg, from the neighborhood, Barry Freedman, from another neighborhood close by, and I would meet often to hang out and go exploring. We'd go over to a busy road nearby, stick our thumbs out, and when someone stopped to give us a ride, we all piled in. The usual question from the driver was "Where you going?", but we generally countered with the same question and were content to be dropped off wherever the driver was going. Once there, we wandered around the environs we found ourselves in, often walking four abreast down the sidewalk, our arms around each others' shoulders, simply looking for adventure and taking in the sights and smells of another part of Baltimore that was new to us. The Four Musketeers.

In hitchhiking around town, I was following a grander version of that activity that my oldest brothers had engaged in. Both Leonard and Billy hitchhiked across the country when they were in their teens. Of course, hitchhiking then was not as dangerous as it later became. By the time my friends and I took to touring around Baltimore, it had gotten to be a little more "iffy." Whenever the guys and I met for a night of hitchhiking all over Baltimore, I gave my parents a vague response to their question of what I was doing and where I was going. I gave just as vague an accounting the next day of where I had been if they asked. While aware of the possibility of danger in going all over the city in strangers' cars, as we did, we felt there was strength in our numbers. Nothing unsafe or untoward ever did happen in all these wide-ranging explorations, but looking back on it now, I see how foolhardy it was. My parents would have fainted if they knew what we were doing, where we were going, and how we were getting there.

My closest friend during those years was not a part of this group. Abraham "Ace" Charrick was the son of a rabbi. Abe's father was born in Lithuania and in many ways did not appear to countenance the newfangled ways and mores of this country. He was the rabbi of Keser Torah congregation on Park Heights Avenue and, as if in illustration of how closely he embraced the religion, lived in the house next door to his *shul*. Abe's parents followed the rituals of Orthodox Judaism strictly and insisted that all their children do the same. Their family composition was the opposite of mine, gender-wise: four girls and one boy, Abe.

Abe chafed at the strictures his parents imposed on their children. He and I soon found ourselves to be good, compatible friends, sharing our innermost thoughts about our lives and loves as well as our ideas and dreams. We hitchhiked to record hops around the northwest section of the city in search of girls and dance partners. As strict as Abe's father was, even he often opened the meeting hall of his *shul* for some of these dances on Saturday nights after the Jewish Sabbath had ended, donating the admission proceeds to various charities.

Another teenage haunt Abe and I often patronized was the Crest movie theater and the nearby Hilltop Diner. After the evening movie ended at the Crest on a Saturday night, the Hilltop could always be counted on to fill with teens from all over northwest Baltimore, hanging out over hamburgers and sodas. The Hilltop is purported to have served as the inspiration for the film *Diner* by Barry Levinson, another Baltimore boy from about that era. Abe and I would keep our ears open at the diner for mention of parties that other kids had heard about and then crash them. We especially liked to go to parties on upper Park Heights Avenue, an area geographically and several socieconomic strata north of Abe's and mine. We were assured of finding pretty girls there, their noses in the air—figuratively as if in demonstration of their superiority and literally as if in demonstration of the nose jobs they had gotten to make themselves look more mainstream.

One of the milestones Abe and I experienced together was the city's parade to celebrate its minor league Baltimore Orioles baseball club's entrance into the American League. As little of a sports fan as I am, seeing that parade with him stays in my mind as being present at a momentous celebration.

At the height of our friendship, Abe entered a yeshiva in Cleveland to study. When I entered Hopkins in 1954, and we found ourselves in totally different environments and states, our friendship withered.

8

IF YOU CAN'T BE AN ATHLETE . . .

"Just play. Have fun. Enjoy the game."
— Michael Jordan

O N REACHING MY teen years, fun and games with my friends turned to more recognized recreational endeavors: basketball, softball, and football. One of the local synagogues, Beth Jacob, much farther out of the city, had a gym that it opened to kids who wanted to play basketball. Many of us in the neighborhood took them up on it, hitchhiking out to it a couple nights a week, our sneakers tied together and slung jauntily over our shoulders. We played in our street clothes, as there were no changing facilities, leaving and returning home sweaty and smelly. I didn't have the requisite height to be a very effective basketball player. Plus, the game bored me. Dribble-dribble-dribble-shoot seemed to me to be all it consisted of—over and over again.

There weren't any sandlot baseball teams in our neck of the woods. We played softball, instead, at a playground outside of the neighborhood that also required hitchhiking to get to. I generally played shortstop, for no particular reason as I had no greater talent for that position over any others. We had no coach nor anyone to direct us, so it was pretty much catch as catch can (so to speak). On arriving at the playground's diamond, we would either choose up sides among ourselves and play a game or two or find another team there to play against.

The neighborhood boys played football in the adjoining back yards behind the Woodbrook Avenue apartment houses. After a few months of pickup football games, we decided to give ourselves a team name. Charlie had played on a neighborhood football team called the Westbury Wildcats a few years before, but when his teammates began to move away or go on to bigger and better things—like girls—that team disintegrated. To honor the glory of that former neighborhood team, we also called ourselves the Westbury Wildcats. An older boy who had played on the original Westbury Wildcats noticed us practicing in the back yards one day and decided to take us under his wing to coach us. After a while, he took us big time, so to speak, and entered us into a sandlot football league playing teams from all over Baltimore. We were the new Westbury Wildcats, and I played right end!

One day at practice on the Druid Hill Park grass, upon catching a pass in one of our intrasquad scrimmages, I was tackled by a teammate, Warren Schwartz. Warren had at least six inches of height on me as well as several pounds. I don't recall what happened in the ensuing half-minute, for he had knocked me unconscious—my second bout of unconsciousness in my young life. We didn't know about concussions in those days, and no adults attended our practices to direct us anyway, so I continued playing after a rest period of a minute or so. Warren went on to play football for Western Maryland College and, after that, had a career as a football and basketball coach at various schools around Baltimore.

After our first season, our "coach," the older boy who organized us to begin with, managed to pull off a real coup: He got the Charles Antell Company, a now-defunct Baltimore manufacturer of hair products for men, to sponsor us. The half-hour-long TV commercials for the company's Charles

Antell Formula No. 9 lanolin-based product were played all over Baltimore and beyond at the time. They declaimed "Folks, have you ever seen a bald-headed sheep? Well, I'm here to tell you that sheep produce lanolin and that's why you will have a beautiful head of hair if you use Formula No. 9 . . . . " As sponsor of our football team, the Charles Antell Company out-fitted us with full football uniforms in the company's iconic crimson color: football pants with a thin white stripe down the side, shoul-der pads, helmets, and jerseys with "Charles Antell" emblazoned on the front. We weren't that great, but, boy, did we look sharp in our Charles Antell uniforms!

One of our football games had the Westbury Wildcats pitted against the Red Shield Boys Club, a team from the tough High-landtown section of Baltimore. The Red Shields had a reputation for playing dirty and for having a bunch of anti-Semites on the team, to boot. Since the Wildcats comprised mostly Jewish kids from our neighborhood, we faced the game with fear and trep-idation. True to form, the Red Shielders played dirty, dropped a few slurs on us "Jew boys," and won the game.

I continued on as an end with the Westbury Wildcats in a not terribly stellar football career. It was a way to hang out with the guys and burn off energy. And we sure looked fine in our crimson uniforms.

I don't know whether it was the near-concussion I received at Warren Schwartz's hands (and body and feet) during that football practice, the fact that I was always the shortest boy on the basketball court at Beth Jacob and thought the game was boring anyway, or that I was always one of the last chosen in a pickup softball game, but whatever it was, I knew that a career as a professional athlete was not going to be mine. So, as the old joke goes, if you can't be an athlete, be an athletic supporter.

As Charlie was on the cheerleading squad when he attended Baltimore Polytechnic Institute several years before me, I, too, went out for cheerleading when I entered Poly, and I made it onto the squad. I enjoyed leading cheers at the football games Poly played against the other Baltimore public high schools.

Charlie, my cheerleader inspiration, went on, by the way, to become a cheerleader for Baltimore's professional football team, the Baltimore Colts. This was back in the day before pro football cheerleading squads consisted entirely of pretty, nubile young women—he wouldn't have made it onto the squad if that standard had been in place—and also, on another historical note, prior to the time the Colts were spirited out of Baltimore in the dead of night to become the Indianapolis Colts.

Although I was finally starting to experience an adolescent growth spurt after I entered college, I was still two or three years younger than most of my classmates, so, by comparison, I was too small (not to mention too ill-coordinated) to go out for any sports at Johns Hopkins. My extra-curricular activities there consisted of going out for cheerleading (and soon becoming head cheerleader); being secretary of the Boosters Club and a member of the H-Club, both of which clubs had as their purpose instilling school spirit; and serving on the Athletic Awards Board. On the non-sports front, along with classmate Merrill Berman, I also co-founded the Johns Hopkins chapter of Psi Chi, the national honorary society in psychology, and I subsequently became the chapter president.

9

THIS WORKING LIFE

"We don't always get the kind of work we want,
but we always have a choice of whether to do it
with good grace or not."

— Sir Christopher Lee

G ROWING UP AS THE youngest of five children among
family members who were busy and industrious, I saw
everyone in the house always gainfully occupied. My brothers
and sister were usually either studying or working. Or both—
all three of my brothers at some point in their lives attended
night school while holding down jobs during the day (or vice
versa). And my parents were notoriously hard workers. Dad's
long hours were legendary. So were Mom's. Since her work
was raising our family of five children, full time, at home, I
could see firsthand how long and hard she worked at it.

My earliest "outside" jobs were as a newspaper delivery
boy, jobs that I held at ages 10 and 11. Charlie had worked as a
newsboy for one of Baltimore's local papers, hopping on streetcars to hawk the day's edition to the riders, then hopping off
when he had worked his way from the front to the back of the
car. It was customary in those days for streetcar operators not
to demand fares from itinerant newsboys who went on and off

their vehicles hawking papers. My parents did not like the fact that Charlie was doing that, and they raised a fuss about it. But delivering newspapers along an established neighborhood route did not seem nearly so perilous to them or to me, so I decided to speak to the adult route manager for the *Baltimore Sun* about delivering papers. I was shortly hired to deliver newspapers to homes in and around the neighborhood.

My route consisted of all of Auchentroly Terrace from Fulton Avenue—where the elementary school I attended as a younger boy was located—north to its end near my house, and then all the streets in my immediate neighborhood. Daily I would pick up the papers that were left in a wired bundle in a Fulton Avenue storefront, snip the wires, place the papers in a sling provided by the *Sunpapers*, and walk toward home, folding each paper into a small packet that I would throw at the door of each customer on my route as I walked by. Because the *Sun*'s manager had acquired all these customers, and then collected money monthly from them for the papers that I delivered to them, I was simply the means of delivery of their daily *Baltimore Evening Sun* and was paid a small amount for each one I delivered. I found out some years later that my parents were not at all thrilled by my walking alone along my paper route, and a few times early in my paper delivery "career" my father shadowed me, unbeknown to me, to make sure I was not hurt or bothered along the way.

After several months of working for the *Sun*, I decided I wanted to earn more for my efforts, so, on the advice of some of my friends, I spoke to the neighborhood delivery manager for the *Baltimore Sun*'s rival newspaper, the *Baltimore American*. The *American* had a different system: In addition to actually delivering the papers, the *American*'s newspaper delivery boys did all the work that the *Sun*'s manager did in landing customers and collecting money from them for the papers. As a delivery boy, it was up to me to canvass my route to get customers to agree to home delivery of the *American*. And as a delivery boy,

I bought the papers I needed from the *American* at a wholesale price, delivered them, and then, once a week, collected the retail price from my customers, keeping the difference as my pay. Boy, I thought when I started with the *American*, I'll get to earn a lot more.

What I didn't count on were several factors that led to my bringing home a lot less. The *American* had a smaller circulation (at least in my neighborhood) than the *Sun*, and my customers were not at all hesitant to stiff an 11-year-old boy—often not answering the door when I went to collect or telling me to "come back next week because we're short of money this week." The biggest problem, however, was mine alone—the irresistible urge I had after I had finished collecting from my customers to throw my collection money down the drain by playing the pinball machines at Sachs's Drug Store.

A saving grace of the job delivering for the *Baltimore American* came out of the blue one day when I was out collecting on Gwynns Falls Parkway. As I passed one of the houses (not one of my customers'), I heard the most soulful, harmonic gospel music coming from the open door. I stopped outside the open door, absolutely transfixed, to listen to the black singing group inside making a joyful sound as they sang *Peace in the Valley*. When one of the singers spied me, he invited me in, and I stayed in their kitchen for 15 minutes listening to them. I don't know whether or not they were professionals practicing or just friends who got together to sing, but they produced a vibrant gospel sound that any group of gospel singers would have been proud to call their own. I discovered subsequently that if I timed it just right on my weekly collection rounds, I could often be treated to their singing. Kind of made up for the fact that I netted so little money plying that delivery route.

My real jobs, the sort that involved formal pay for formal work, started a few years later. Not long ago I perused a form sent to me by the Social Security Administration that showed my lifetime earnings for those real jobs. The earliest entries in that earnings history caught my eye: 1954, $283; 1955, $497; 1956, $595. This brought me back to the summer jobs of my youth.

In the summer of 1954, in my 15th year, I graduated from Baltimore City College. I had been accepted to the only under-graduate institution to which I applied, The Johns Hopkins University, and before I started there, I needed to work during the summer to earn as much of the $800 per year tuition that I could. While I wanted a job, I dreaded having to look for one. My previous jobs serving newspapers more or less came to me, rather than I to them, and they were not "real" jobs, anyway, just spending money jobs. For a small, shy, awkward 15-year-old, the thought of putting myself forward to some strange adult in order to land a summer position was terrifying. I remember my mother saying, in that impeccable logic mothers have, that if I wanted a summer job, I'd have to go out and find one. So I turned to the classified ads in the newspapers, the main way to find out in the mid-1950s what jobs were available. I dutifully circled the jobs in the classified ads I thought I might have a chance at landing, timorously called to make appointments with the adult voices on the other end, and then hopped a bus to East Baltimore, downtown Baltimore, Edmonson Village—wherever there was someone willing to give a squeaky-voiced, frightened 15-year-old a job interview. Beating the pavements for a few days went quickly from frightening to frightening and wearying.

The telling of two lies was instrumental in getting the job I finally landed that summer at Claymore C. Sieck Wholesale Florist. As a minor, I needed to get a work permit in order to be legally sanctioned to work, but even for a minor's work permit, I had to be at least 16 years old. I reported this to my mother, who said she would take me to the Baltimore Office of Work Permits—or whatever it was called—where, upon facing the clerk, she lied that I was 16 years old. On reflection, I think she didn't flinch at engaging in that lie because, one, she probably was relieved to have me, the youngest of her five children, out of her hair for the summer, and, two, the money I would earn was needed for my college tuition. For my part, I thought that if Mom would lie about my age, it must be at least passably okay to do so. It seemed that a little white lie in the face of rules and regulations—where no real harm would ensue—could occasionally be warranted. Thus, duly, if deceptively, vouched for, I was granted a work permit to begin my first summer job.

I was a stockboy-janitor there, working Monday through Saturday for the munificent sum of 40 cents an hour. You can do the math to see how many hours I had to work to add up to the $283 reported on my Social Security statement for that year.

In the course of working there, I came to learn that Claymore C. Sieck Wholesale Florist was the second largest wholesale florist in all of Baltimore. Back then, its operation in that single Baltimore location employed maybe 25 people, tops. Today, the Sieck Company employs over 350 people in its 10 locations in the northeastern United States to serve more than 2,500 retail florists. And I was there on the ground floor (literally) of that growth.

Sieck's was in an old brick building that rose four stories above Calvert Street on the edge of downtown. All the floral distribution activity took place on the ground floor, where I mainly worked. It consisted of a large open area with dark wooden floors, a loft for storing shipping cartons and other supplies, and a cold room for the flowers. The second floor held the offices of Mr. Claymore Sieck and his son, Bill Sieck, and a few other workers. I never did find out what was on the floors above those.

My job was to keep the floors, sinks, and packing tables of the distribution area clean of debris; keep the inventory rotated in the cold room so that no flower bunches would get too old; fold and staple the boxes—large 4- by 2- by 2-foot corrugated packing boxes—in which the orders would be placed; and even—a small triumph of the summer—help pack some orders.

Frank and Ed, brothers, were the salesmen. They took the orders from the retail florists who visited us several times a week to make their selections. These salesmen were also responsible for seeing to it that the boxes packed with the flowers that were going to their customers were filled properly—flowers fresh and of the type and quantity ordered, and packed so as to survive the trip by truck to the retailers who ordered them. Frank was the bane of my existence that summer. A fussy man, he was forever on my neck for not stapling the packing boxes to his liking (note I didn't say stapling them correctly), not keeping the cold room to his liking (note I didn't say in order), and, the worst sin, not treating the Fuji mums as gently as he would treat them (okay, here I was guilty).

Fuji mums are spectacular plants with heavy heads of long, lacy flower petals on long, thin stems. Their heavy heads are particularly prone to separating from their stems if not handled with the utmost delicacy. When packing them, I had to make pillows of rolled newspapers to put under the stems to help cradle their fragile heads. Frank could handle Fuji mums with the required utmost delicacy. I, not very well-coordinated, could not. Several times that summer, I accidentally separated some Fuji mum heads from their Fuji mum bodies. Frank would fly into a fit at these accidental beheadings. I tried as little as possible to handle Fuji mums—rather difficult to achieve, given their popularity among the retailers—and as little as possible to come into contact with Frank.

Another lowlight of that summer was not a person—most of the other people at Sieck's treated me well—but rather a flower or, more precisely, a flower species. Gardenias were more popular then as a florist flower than they are now, and we stocked dozens of them at all times. Gardenias have a scent that to me is cloying even when they are fresh. Rotten gardenias, though, emit an odor beyond description. And flowers did go downhill at Sieck's if they stocked more than the retailers bought each week. Every Saturday, at the end of the work week, one of my tasks was to go through the inventory of flowers in the cold room and throw out any that were even slightly past their prime, on the premise that they would not be fresh enough to be saleable come Monday of the following week. Many a time I came upon gardenias that were past their prime, and when gardenias go downhill, they go downhill fast. The odor of rotten gardenias sickens me, and to this day, I shun gardenias, no matter how fresh. Even their fresh aroma reminds me of what that scent could deteriorate to.

Mr. Sieck told me that I could take home any flowers I was throwing out for the weekend that I wanted. I certainly took him up on it, and most Saturdays I came home from my job bearing orchids, roses, and mums—but never gardenias—that were a bit off-peak, but still presentable. Our house was filled with flowers every weekend that summer, thanks to Mr. Sieck's generous spirit. The girlfriend of my youth, Quinn, was likewise showered with flowers on the weekends.

The work was hard—sweeping the floors, cleaning the sinks, making up delivery boxes, going from the main distribution and packing floor (un-air conditioned in Baltimore's typical 90 degree, 90 percent humidity summer days) into the cold room (where the temperature was always in the 40s) to get flowers out, and sometimes staying in the cold room for long periods to rotate the stock and put the shelves in order. Each day, I brought the lunch Mom packed for me and would either take a stroll outside to sit on a curb on nearby Calvert Street to eat it or sit on the loft stairs to munch my sandwich. One of the packers was Stubby, a short, sweet man who worked hard and uncomplainingly. He introduced me to the practice of lying down to rest after eating lunch on the pallet of flat, as-yet-unmade corrugated cardboard packing boxes in the loft, as he often did. I believe that that was the beginning of my lifelong ability, which stood me in good stead in graduate school, to take a short nap in the middle of the day and awaken refreshed and able to work more hours more efficiently than I would otherwise be able to do.

Another thing I learned from Stubby was something even more practical that I retain to this day, namely, how to tie a Parcel Post knot. All the outgoing order boxes were tied with this knot, so if I was to learn to prepare a box of flowers for shipment, I had to learn to tie that kind of knot. I won't burden you with the details of how to tie one, but it is simple to do and extremely useful to know. A Parcel Post knot allows you to circumnavigate a box in one direction with rope or twine, tighten it so that it remains tight, and then circumnavigate the box with the twine at right angles to the first course of twine, then secure the box smartly with a final knot. Of all the new things I did that summer, learning from Stubby how to tie a Parcel Post knot was the one that had the longest lasting everyday value.

One day that summer, the younger Mr. Sieck introduced me to some basic research the company was funding. Back then, there was no way to preserve cut flowers out of water and still retain permanently their original life-like color and texture. I don't think that even today a way has been found. Mr. Sieck had hired a man who worked, by himself, on the second floor in a sort of office-lab combined, trying to figure out how to solve that puzzle. I suppose the company that figured that one out would either make a fortune from the process or patent it to keep anyone else from using it and ruining the fresh flower industry. Mr. Sieck took me to the lab and left me with the man so I could see what he was doing and ask him questions. Here was no mad scientist, but rather a trained chemist doing serious work. I remember spending a fascinating hour with him as he explained the various roads he had followed, showed me the results of some of his experiments—none of them completely successful—and answered my questions. I think that, in a measurable way, that hour contributed to my fascination with the way science works and to my choice ultimately to become a researcher.

The worst part of the summer of '54 was the three days I

spent with the Christmas wreaths. Even though the outside weather was in the 90s, in the wholesale trade you had to think ahead, and the Siecks, of course, were thinking ahead to winter when they ordered a boxcar full of boxed artificial Christmas wreaths. When the boxcar arrived in July at a railroad siding next to the nearby Maryland penitentiary, it naturally had to be unloaded into a truck and the truck driven three blocks away to the storage warehouse two buildings up from the Sieck establishment. That job fell to me and two men that Sieck's hired from off the streets—one an unshaven, unkempt gray-haired man in his fifties, the other a thirtyish, burly street person.

You cannot know, looking at one from the outside, how much a boxcar holds until you've seen the inside of one. That one boxcar must have held ten thousand boxes of wreaths. For three days, my two compatriots-in-misery and I unloaded boxes of wreaths, stacked them in a truck, hauled them to the warehouse, unloaded them, stacked them in the warehouse, and then drove the truck back the few blocks to the railroad siding to do it all over again. I'll never forget the two street guys slaking their thirst those long, hot, miserable days that summer (did I mention yet that Baltimore has long, hot, miserable summer days?) using a rusty tin can they found in the alley to dip into a puddle of water in the alley. Thirsty as I was at times, I passed on quenching my thirst that way.

To make the whole miserable task even more miserable, the three of us had to do it under the eye of the evil supervisor, whose name I have mercifully forgotten but whose face haunts me still. The man would think nothing—perhaps because he could not think at all—of having us build a stack of 50 boxes of wreaths going from the warehouse floor to its ceiling, and then telling us that he decided he wanted us to dismantle the stack and restack the wreaths four feet over to the left. That happened more than occasionally; only the distances and directions changed. It took everything I could muster to keep from telling him what an unthinking, sadistic s.o.b. he was.

The summer ended, and I had earned my $283, which was at least a dent in my tuition at Hopkins. I had learned much in that first summer job: That if you want something, you have to work hard for it; that if you work hard, you will be rewarded for your good work (even if it is only 40 cents an hour); that often you have to bite your tongue and keep silent in the face of unreasonableness; that scientific inquiry can be fascinating; and, of course, that knowing how to tie a Parcel Post knot is one of the most valuable practical bits of knowledge a person can possess.

In order to get that summer job in the first place, I hadn't told the Siecks I was going to college in the fall (here's that second lie). They wouldn't have hired me, I reasoned, if they had known I was going to leave three months later. So one day in August, I screwed up my courage and went up to Mr. Bill Sieck, who always treated me well, to tell him that I had just been accepted unexpectedly to Johns Hopkins and that, regretfully, I would have to leave the employ of Claymore C. Sieck Wholesale Florist. Looking back over the distance of a half century, I think that the Messrs. Sieck really suspected all along that I was college bound and that I would not be in their employ for much longer than the summer. That assumption on my part was confirmed for me when I saw news not long ago that the Greater Baltimore Committee honored Claymore C. Sieck Wholesale Florist for providing tuition and summer jobs for students in the Baltimore area.

The next two weeks after my meeting with the junior Mr. Sieck were a bit sad, saying goodbye to Stubby, Ed (but not Frank), the women in the office, and Bill and Claymore Sieck. On my last day there, the elder Mr. Sieck, also a kindly man, called me into his office and said a few inspirational words about starting out in college. Then, to my surprise, he pulled out a small gift box and solemnly presented a parting gift to me. It was a tie clip in the shape of a monkey wrench. Perhaps he thought that, attending a university with a good engineering school, I was going to become an engineer. Or perhaps it was his subtle way of saying that I had done such a good job at the company that summer that my departure was throwing a wrench into the whole enterprise. I like to think it was the latter.

———————

After my first year at Johns Hopkins, the university did award me small partial tuition grants, but I still had to earn money in the summers toward the rest of my tuition. So, prior to my sophomore year, I landed a summer-only job at a carry-out seafood shop on 25th Street in Baltimore. The shop was a present that a father, a Mr. Stanley, gave to his two grown sons, one of whom was a teacher, to provide them with summer employment and income. The word "seafood" in Baltimore means, first and foremost, crabs—steamed blue point crabs. Google "blue point crab" even now and at least a half dozen seafood houses with that name alone in Maryland will come up. One of my very first tasks upon being hired was to help finish off a plaster-of-Paris construction, some five feet high and representing a crab, that stood outside the store to announce the establishment to the world. This was no flat, two-dimensional sign, but a three-dimensional giant crab painted bright red, the color of a steamed crab. Furthermore, they had rigged it with an electric motor so that its claw moved back and forth rhythmically (and eerily), beckoning people to come in to Stanley's Carry-Out House of Seafood. It certainly grabbed people's attention as they passed along 25th Street.

My main function, at least initially that summer, was to work in the kitchen steaming the crabs. This entailed going into the cold room (another cold room!), taking a couple of bushel baskets of live crabs to the kitchen, and there placing each live crab, one-by-one and right side up, on a rack at the bottom of a large cooking vat. Beneath the rack at the bottom of the pot we poured stale beer to steam the crabs in. This being

Maryland, we then poured atop each layer of crabs a pepper-based spice, Old Bay Seafood Seasoning—lots and lots of it. That summer I had the worst case of poison ivy I ever had, and my arms oozed from the poison ivy blisters. When I poured the Old Bay on, clouds of it arose to attack my arms, raw as they were with poison ivy blisters and sores, to make the itching a living hell.

In Baltimore's summers, the temperature regularly hit 100 degrees, with the humidity approaching that same number, or at least it felt that way. The temperature *inside* the kitchen, often with three or four vats of crabs steaming away at once, regularly hit 120 degrees Fahrenheit. One of my co-workers for the summer, Dave Scudder, was a portly lad a little older than I. As we sweated our days away in the kitchen, I could tell that Dave was liking the job less and less. Finally, after working at it for only a couple of weeks, he announced his intention to quit. "Why?" I asked him.

"Because I actually see myself dripping away down the drain every day I work in this goddamned kitchen," was poor Dave's reply.

After he left, Dave was replaced by two Korean brothers in their early 20s who had served recently in the South Korean Army. This was 1955, a couple of years after the Korean War armistice came about. The brothers were likeable chaps who spoke no English, but at least they had each other to talk to. With signs and gestures, I showed them how to steam the crabs. In appreciation, they in turn taught me the words and music of a classic Korean folk song, *Arirang*. To this day, 60 years later, I still remember the Korean lyrics and can do a creditable job of singing the song. This is how I remember the words they taught me:

Arirang, Arirang, Arariyo.
Arirang gogeddo, nomo ganda.
Na'di podego,
Kasina nimun.

Shimni do mokaso,

Pal pyang yan da.

With the kitchen well-covered by the Korean brothers, the Stanley boys, as I called the other pair of brothers, reassigned me to other tasks. One was to drive their panel truck every morning to Annapolis to pick up a load of live crabs from a crab fisherman with whom they had arranged to buy a daily quota of crabs. This arrangement was likely off the books on both sides of the bargain.

Imagine the pride and sense of self-importance I had—having only recently turned 16 and gotten my driver's license—driving that panel truck every day the 30 miles from Baltimore to Annapolis and back. Those return trips provided some dramatic moments, too. The crabber delivered the wriggling, jiggling crabs to me in bushel baskets made of thin wood slats, with a similarly constructed top affixed to each basket by wires. The wire latches, such as they were, were not foolproof, though, and on many of my trips back to Baltimore, crabs escaped and made their way up to me at the driver's seat. Sometimes, I tried to reach down and grab the errant crabs to shove them back into their baskets as I drove, but a few well-delivered pinches from the crabs' claws to the web of skin between my thumb and forefinger, and a few sudden swerves of the truck, convinced me to stop the truck to capture the crabs and return them to their baskets. These escapes provided exciting moments on the road.

Despite my close and extended encounters with these animals, I never lost my liking for steamed crabs. Their seafood-like aroma mixed with the smell of the sea itself makes my mouth water. When it does, I can almost taste the piquancy of the red pepper sprinkled on their shells that mixes with the meat inside when I crack them open and pick out the succulent white meat to put in my mouth.

Since my driving to and from Annapolis consumed only the better part of each morning, I was usually assigned to wait on customers at the counter for the rest of the day. Once steamed, the crabs, whose shells turned from blue to red in the steaming process, were taken from the vats and placed on wire racks in the front of the store for customers to view. There I would meet customers and fill their orders by placing the requested number and type of crabs—small, medium, large, and jumbo—in paper bags for them to take out.

One of the neighborhood girls took to hanging around when I was up front at the shop. She was a tough cookie, mildly attractive and with a nubile body that spoke of pleasures to be savored. She glommed onto the high school ring I wore and, after a time, asked me if I wanted to give it to her, the giving of which would symbolize that we were, in the parlance of the day, "going steady." As young and naïve as I was, even I could see that all she was interested in was capturing a trophy ring she could brag about to her friends. So I kept my high school ring. And my virginity.

———•◦•———

The next summer I worked as a stockboy at Raymond's Store for Men and Boys in Dundalk, a store run, again, by two brothers, Raymond and Sylvin Sass. Dundalk was a foreign country to me, located as it was on the diagonally opposite end of Baltimore from where I lived. The only way I would take that job was if the brothers drove me to it, which they agreed to do. Every morning, I dutifully walked the mile to my pickup point on the corner of West Cold Spring Lane and Pimlico Road to await the brothers as they drove in from their residences farther out. They spent the half-hour it took to drive to their store talking about business and family affairs while I sat in the back absorbed in my own thoughts.

My tasks at Raymond's Store for Men and Boys were similar to my tasks at Sieck's Wholesale Florist, although a lot cleaner and a lot less smelly: keeping the store neat and clean, making sure the pants and shirts on display for sale in the store were neatly arranged, and doing the same for the stock in the rear stockroom. When the summer was about two-thirds gone, the brothers told me I could wait on customers who walked in if they themselves were busy with other customers. After a few brief lessons on how to wait on customers and measure them for alterations, I was unleashed on an unsuspecting public. I am not a very forward or gifted salesperson, nor am I a clothes horse by any means, but I guess Raymond and Sylvin thought I could at least help out in a pinch.

One customer experience I had that summer stands out in my mind. The customer came in to buy some trousers. I showed him one pair, then another, then still other ones for him to assess, try on, and decide among. Each time he finished trying on a pair, I put it aside until five pairs had piled up. He picked out two pairs to buy and put each on again for me to mark with tailor's chalk where the cuffs were to go and where the seat was to be let out. Just as he was about to leave, though, he told me he decided he would take only one of the pairs of pants, which he pointed out to me. When he came in to the store a week later to pick up the pair of pants after it had been altered to his length and body, I boxed his purchase, handed him the box, and he paid and left.

A week after that, he returned to the store in a rage. I was in the stockroom and not visible, but I could hear what was going on out front. The customer complained loudly to Raymond that he had been given the wrong pair of pants, and he demanded his money back. In those days of independent stores and independent owners, "the customer is always right" ethos was not necessarily always practiced. Raymond, not wanting to see a sale vanish from his books, took the position that this customer was *not* right. He *was* given the correct pair of pants, Raymond insisted just as loudly, and the store would not take the pants back or refund the customer his money. Essentially, Raymond told him to take a hike.

Cowering in the back, listening to the customer ranting and Raymond ranting back, I searched my memory to ascertain if I might, indeed, have sent the wrong pair of marked-up pants to the tailor. I concluded I might have. There was that pile of trousers that he had tried on and two that I marked up for him—I could easily have gotten things mixed up (and possibly did). Raymond never spoke to me about this incident, and I sure didn't want to bring it up. But in retrospect I wonder if, even though he was a hard-headed businessman, he decided not to injure the fragile confidence of a 17-year-old boy and instead back me up on the transaction

The summer before my senior year at Hopkins, Uncle Len came to my rescue from summer job hell by offering to have me work for him that summer. As Director of the Division of Statistics and Epidemiology of the National Institute of Neurological Diseases and Blindness—later renamed the National Institute of Neurological Disorders and Stroke—Leonard T. Kurland was a highly respected research physician in the forefront of public health and epidemiological investigations of disorders such as amyotrophic lateral sclerosis, myasthenia gravis, multiple sclerosis, kuru, kwashiorkor, and glaucoma. By the time he died in 1995, he was the author or co-author of 523 publications in medical and scientific journals. My 30 publications over my lifetime in similar kinds of journals pale by comparison to Uncle Len's impressive accomplishment.

Since Uncle Len's offices were in Silver Spring, Maryland, just outside of Washington, I lived with my sister Margie and her husband Lenny at their house in Silver Spring for the summer. The job immersed me in what it meant to be a researcher full-time, and it solidified the leanings I already had that scientific research was what I wanted to do. Seeing that this was the direction in which I was headed, Len put me to work that summer unwrapping diseased human brains sent in from the field for examination, helping synthesize and analyze epidemiological data, attending seminars, and contributing to reports.

Uncle Leonard possessed the rare asset of treating children and adolescents as something more than unknowing nonentities, giving them major responsibilities where other adults would have ignored their potential. He never seemed to doubt that I could handle the important responsibilities he gave me; he considered it natural for intelligent children to be able to do so.

That summer at NINDB I served on the study team to evaluate a new, and supposedly superior, instrument someone had invented to detect glaucoma. Rather than assessing directly the level of pressure in the eyeball by placing a device, the widely used Schiotz Tonometer, directly on the eyeball, this new device, the "Phosphenator," did not require physical contact with the eyeball at all. Instead, it passed a mild electric current through the temples of the patient, who then compared the visual images he or she perceived—the phosphenes—as a result of the current passing through their frontal lobes to a set of images on cards shown to him or her. If the patient selected certain card images as similar to the ones he had perceived when the current was passed through, he or she was said, according to the test, to have glaucoma. Had this new device worked, it would have led to a much more comfortable and tolerable way to diagnose glaucoma, and perhaps better and earlier detection of it. But that was not to be, we discovered.

Assessing patients at the Walter Reed Army Medical Center who had visual problems, our study compared the results of "Phosphenator" measurements to the results of measurements using the standard Schiotz Tonometer, and we found that the Phosphenator did not hold up well at all in detecting glaucoma. I helped run the subjects in the study, record the patient measurements, analyze the data, and write a partial first draft of a journal article. My contributions to this study were rewarded by receiving a junior authorship on the published article: Kurland, L.T., Sachs, D., Kerpelman, L.C., and Davis, F.S., Jr. "Evaluation of the 'Phosphenator' device: For the detection of increased intraocular pressure." *American Journal of Ophthalmology*, 1958, vol. 45, pp. 272-276. Once the article was published a year later, I was thrilled to be able to say that I had, at age 19, a scientific paper in a respected peer-reviewed medical journal to my name—even if that name appeared third out of the four co-authors.

———•••———

What summer job could be better? except my next part-time job. Psychology was my field, and despite the wonderful experience I had that summer at NINDB, I wanted to go into psychological or behavioral research, not medicine or medical research. The summer after my junior year at Johns Hopkins University, a classmate and fellow psychology major, Roger McKinley, told me he was planning to leave his part-time school year job at the Henry Phipps Psychiatric Clinic of The Johns Hopkins Hospital at the end of that summer. He thought I might want to apply to be his replacement. Did I ever!

I contacted Roger's supervisor at Phipps, the psychologist Stanley D. Imber—who, incidentally, had received his doctorate from The University of Rochester a few years earlier—and went down to the Johns Hopkins medical campus in East Baltimore to meet him in order to apply for the job. Dr. Imber—who quickly became Stan—was a psychologist on the interdisciplinary Group Therapy Research team. This unit within the Phipps Clinic was headed by psychiatrist Jerome D. Frank and had on its staff another research psychiatrist, Lester H. Gliedman; two psychologists, Stanley D. Imber and Earl H. Nash; and social worker Anthony R. (Tony) Stone. The name for the group was something of a misnomer, as it did not conduct research solely on group therapy but on many types of psychotherapy. It was among the pioneer groups to apply scientific methodology to the study of psychotherapy. Nonetheless, the name had stuck.

After that initial interview with Stan, at which I queried him as much about graduate work at The University of Rochester as he did me about my background and qualifications for the job, he offered it to me starting part-time as soon as my senior year at Hopkins was to begin in September. I was told it could possibly continue, if I worked out, full-time over the following summer until I was to leave for graduate school. Stan told me that, before I started working for him, I should bone up on "norm-parametric statistics," which his group used extensively to analyze their research data.

Having just been offered a job where I would be doing statistical analysis, I did not want to show my lack of familiarity with the type of statistics he said they used. But since both the words "norm" and "parametric" were common terms in the psychological research literature, I figured that, in the several weeks before I started work, I could get myself up to speed on "norm-parametric statistics." Try as I might to discover what it was all about, though, I could not find a single reference to it in all the books and libraries I searched. I finally had to confess to Stan, when I visited his office a couple of weeks before starting the job, that I did not know what "norm-parametric statistics" was and could find no references to it.

"I'm surprised you couldn't," Stan replied. "It's not an uncommon statistical approach. Here are a few references you can read up on before you start here." He then wrote down the references and handed me his note. As I looked at what he wrote, it became clear that what he was talking about was *non*-parametric statistics, but his native Boston-area accent was so pronounced that it came out, when my brain processed it, as the strange term I had spent weeks trying to find more about, "norm-parametric statistics."

I spent my senior year in college and the summer after it working for the Group Therapy Research Unit at the Henry

Phipps Psychiatric Clinic in its elegant 1912 building with marble floors, porches, gardens, and courtyard. During that time, I grew to respect and admire all these men I worked for, men who treated me as a junior colleague and confrere. In addition to my work within the clinic, summarizing and analyzing data and occasionally interviewing patients, during my off-times I prowled the stacks nearby of the Johns Hopkins Hospital's Welch Medical Library, one of the great medical libraries of the world, to look into the many old journals and displays it housed on medicine and the history of medicine.

I also partook of the festive distraction of the annual turtle derby at the Johns Hopkins Hospital. Every spring, medical students, interns, residents, nurses, and others who worked at this world-famous institution, as well as the general public, gather in the courtyard for what has been an annual tradition since 1931. At the annual turtle derby, conducted in several heats, the turtles—borrowed from local turtle farms and returned to them afterward—are placed in the center of a large circle laid out on the courtyard grass and covered with a bushel basket. At the start of each heat, the basket is lifted and the turtles are "encouraged" to race—really, they just lumber—to the white line demarcating the circle's perimeter. Patience is the name of the game in these races.

Late that year, tragedy struck. In a mid-air collision between a Maryland National Guard jet and a Capital Airlines plane over Western Maryland, all the passengers in the Capital Airlines plane were killed. Among them were Lester Gliedman and his wife. I had had little direct experience with the death of someone close to me up to that time. Although some relatives, including, grandparents, had died while I was growing up, my parents tried to shield me from the unpleasantness of death. While I sometimes accompanied them to houses where relatives were *sitting shiva*—the week-long period of mourning immediately after burial wherein relatives and friends gather at the home of the deceased person or that of a close relative—even into my

teen years I had not attended anyone's funeral. When I attended
the memorial service at a Baltimore funeral home for Dr. Gliedman, it was my most direct experience with the death of
someone I knew. I felt great sadness at the loss of so vibrant
and energetic a man. Several years after that, death struck
another member of the team. I found out that Earl Nash had
died while undergoing surgery. I was even more distressed by
Earl's death. The staff member of the research group closest to
me in age, Earl was an extremely friendly, sweet, giving man
whom I liked very much. It was hard for me to imagine him no
longer in this world.

By the end of my time at the Phipps Clinic, I felt increasingly like the professional I hoped to become and increasingly
confident that my predilection for psychology and psychological
research was the right choice. I was sorry to leave so amicable
a work atmosphere, but happy to embark on the graduate studies
that would lead to my chosen professional career.

10

Music Makes My World Go Round

"All deep things are Song. It seems somehow the very central essence of us, Song; as if all the rest were but wrappages and hulls! The primal element of us; of us, and of all things."

— Thomas Carlyle, *Heroes and Hero Worship*

I DON'T HAVE A strong voice, but I can carry a tune. I've taken up a few instruments during my lifetime but have not achieved real proficiency in any. But I have always loved music and almost always have a song or two playing in my head from the time I get up in the morning until I retire at night. I'm not a musician, I have to confess, but I am a music appreciator. I admire people who can produce music with their own hands, voices, and talents. I like all genres of music (with a few exceptions) from Classical to Country.

It probably helped that my parents liked good music. Although she didn't have a strong voice, Mom always hummed a tune as she worked around the house. She felt that her children should appreciate good music, so often she would buy tickets for me to whatever popular musical or operetta was playing downtown at Ford's Theater or the Lyric Theater and go with me or send me alone to see it. I still have fond memories of seeing touring companies' productions of *Annie Get Your Gun* and *South Pacific* on Baltimore stages by the time I was twelve. The most moving experience I had was seeing, when I was in college, *West Side Story* at its pre-Broadway tryout in Washington. A Hopkins classmate of mine, Bobby Spielman, and I went to see it. It was unlike any musical I had ever seen. Its melodies weren't sappy, its lyrics were thoughtful and insightful, and the choreography and staging were creative and highly unusual for the time. At the end of the performance we attended, the audience sat in silence, stunned by what they had just seen and heard, before they burst into thunderous applause. I couldn't even join in that; I remained absolutely transfixed for another five minutes by the experience before I was able even to move.

One of Aunt Helen's several husbands (she had four) was the Concertmaster of the Baltimore Symphony Orchestra. A courtly old-school European and gentle soul, Ilya Scholnick was a warm and kindly presence in Aunt Helen's elegant Druid Park Lake Drive apartment whenever my family visited during my preteen years. On one of those visits, I got to talking with Uncle Ilya about his job as concertmaster, the orchestra, his playing, and his violin.

"Would you like to see my Stradivarius?" he asked me.

"What's a Stradivarius, Uncle Ilya?" I asked him in turn.

"It's a very old and very expensive violin, made many years ago by a master violin maker," Ilya told me.

I got right to the point: "How old, and how expensive?"

Uncle Ilya rose, saying "Here, I'll show you the instrument." He left the room and, a moment later, returned with his violin case. As he opened it, he said, "This instrument is very rare; it was made by a man named Antonio Stradivari almost 200 years ago, and it is worth half a million dollars [and that was in 1950 dollars!]. Would you like to hold it?"

I was floored, but I couldn't. I didn't want to take the chance that I might harm this rare instrument worth more money than I could even imagine. On the few occasions I attended a Baltimore Symphony Orchestra concert and Uncle Ilya had a solo, I could tell how sweetly yet strongly his violin sang.

My sister, Margie, played piano well. On many evenings the family would gather around the dark-stained upright piano we had in our hall near the stairway and sing the popular songs of the day as she played. Charlie at one point took up the ukulele, no doubt influenced by the fact that Arthur Godfrey, whose radio and television shows were extremely popular at the time, often broke out into song accompanying himself on the ukulele. Seeing and hearing my big brother play the instrument, I prevailed upon my parents to buy a ukulele for me so that I could learn to play it. Charlie taught me how, and the Kerpelman Brothers sang many simple ukulele tunes together.

I took piano lessons a few years after Margie did, but I never reached her level of proficiency and ease with that instrument. We learned from the same teacher, Mrs. Norris, who gave lessons at her house. I would dutifully take the bus to her house every week (after not practicing as much as I should have), climb the stairs to her 2nd-floor apartment, my sheet music ensconced in my bookbag, and there receive my piano lesson. Mrs. Norris used to disappear for a while each time I played whatever I was supposed to have learned that week, returning slightly glassy-eyed and smelling ever so slightly of something I could not then discern (but now know what it was). Given my level of piano-playing proficiency, I can't blame her for taking to drink.

I progressed to being able to play a simplified arrangement of Beethoven's *Moonlight Sonata* for my recital with Mrs. Norris. But I abandoned all hope of ever becoming proficient after that (or maybe it was just other activities in my young life that interfered).

In the 1950s, I discovered Rhythm and Blues. Around that time, Bill Haley was popular with his rockabilly music (some say he was the progenitor of Rock and Roll). Like most kids I knew, I liked his music and danced to it (on one occasion, dancing to it live when he appeared with his group, the Comets, at Carlin's Park), but it didn't "hit me where I lived." In twirling the radio dial to find other music, I came upon a station playing tunes that really did hit me where I lived. I could tell from the way the music grooved and the words were pronounced that the artists I was hearing were black, and I really liked what I heard. That music was Rhythm and Blues, and not too many other white kids at the time seemed to know of its existence. I was soon singing along with the likes of The Platters, The Drifters, The Supremes, Little Richard, The Midnighters, The Penguins, and others. Later, I haunted downtown record stores to find and buy 45 RPM phonograph records by these artists.

Before too long, the mainstream (i.e., white) music establishment began to notice this music as well. By the mid-1950s, white artists were coming out with cover versions of black music. My favorite soulful song, *Earth Angel* by The Penguins, was covered by The Crew Cuts, an obviously white singing group with a name that a bunch of white music executives must have thought was "cool." Like most white covers of songs, their rendition was white-bread-awful—dead, soulless, and vanilla plain—but the white teens ate it up.

The biggest offender in my mind of this trend—white artists capitalizing on Rhythm and Blues music—was Pat Boone. Often within months of black singers or groups coming out with R & B hits, Pat Boone would release a cover version of them: Fats Domino's *Ain't That a Shame*, The Platters' *The Great Pretender*, and Little Richard's *Long Tall Sally* and *Tutti Frutti*, to name a few. There were other covers by other white artists, too. The Midnighters' raunchy *Work With Me Annie* was reworked into the more acceptable (for white audiences) *Dance With Me Henry*, put out by Georgia Gibbs; The Spaniels' *Goodnight Sweetheart* was covered by The McGuire Sisters; The "5" Royales' *Dedicated to the One I Love* was covered by the Mamas and the Papas. I forgive the Mamas and the Papas for that one, though. They had the decency to release their version a couple of decades after The "5" Royales' version (plus, I never heard a Mamas and the Papas song I didn't like).

Because the white teenage record buyers for the most part did not even know of the existence of R & B, and because they outnumbered black teenagers, the white covers of R & B songs from people like Pat Boone regrettably swamped the R & B versions in record sales. This was all some years before the morphing of R & B into Rock 'n' Roll, so in those early years, the black artists suffered economically from having their songs and records "stolen" and repurposed to serve the larger white audience. It infuriated me, but it also made me sad that the white kids who bought the white-bread-imitations did not have the experience of hearing the original, more soulful and gutsy, versions of the songs they were listening to. I felt that all the white kids I knew were missing out on some of the greatest music ever played, and I felt special that I had discovered this genre that none of my friends or schoolmates were even aware of.

One of Baltimore's most popular radio personalities among the black population, Hot Rod Hulbert, played R & B music late every night on his hours-long show on radio station WITH. I listened to him whenever I could. Hot Rod had developed a patter and an idiom—"Copacetic," "VOSA" and "Great Googamooga" were a few of his signature utterances indicating his approval of the record he was spinning at the moment—that I thought were the coolest. And the groups whose records he spun were spectacular, pounding out gritty, soulful, driving lyrics and rhythms.

Hot Rod had as one of his regular sponsors Arnold Sales, a furniture and television emporium, whose advertising jingle he played when he aired a commercial for the store. To the tune of "Runnin' Wild," it went:

> Come on down,
> To Arnold Sales,
> It's the place,
> For you and me.
> Talk to Television Tank,
> He's the man, that you should really see . . . and thank!

One night, Hot Rod announced that he would be broadcasting the following week from the window of a furniture store in Baltimore's black section. Since my father was in the furniture business, I asked him if he could get me into the store Hot Rod was scheduled to broadcast from. Dad didn't know the owner of the place, but he could tell I really wanted to do this. He must have made a few phone calls and a few promises, for the next week, he drove me down to the store and we both went in. Hot Rod looked askance at this little white kid and his father invading the sacrosanct broadcast space that was set up for him in the store. The great Hot Rod didn't even deign to acknowledge our presence, but I didn't mind. I was in the presence of my own favorite DJ and my own favorite music. Dad and I stayed for almost an hour, then tip-toed out of the store, silently nodding our thanks to Hot Rod for "sharing" the moment with us. Maurice "Hot Rod" Hulbert, Jr. ultimately was recognized as one of the legendary pioneers of black radio in a book of the same name by Gilbert A. Williams. And I knew him when.

As much as I liked to listen to music, I also liked to dance. But I refused to dance unless I was certain I could master the steps of whatever dance number was being played. I just didn't want to look like an ungraceful fool. I'm not sure how other kids my age learned to dance, but I went to record hops at playgrounds around the city in the summer—sometimes with my friends and sometimes by myself—and lurked in the dark to watch the dancers as they went through their steps. As they did, I did my best to mimic what they were doing until I had gotten the hang of it. Once I did, I felt comfortable asking girls to dance with me.

I soon developed a platonic relationship with one girl in particular, Sue Munaker, because she was a terrific dancer. We would meet at various playground record hops in our part of the city and sometimes enter their dance contests. We won one, too, an accomplishment of which I was inordinately proud. No prize, money, or fame resulted from winning, just bragging rights, but that was enough for me.

While still holding a great love for Rhythm and Blues, my musical tastes soon broadened to jazz. Having become enamored of that musical form, I wanted to learn to play the saxophone. I loved the way each type of sax, whether soprano, alto, tenor, or baritone, sounded. I prevailed upon my parents to rent an alto sax for me at a music store for six weeks. The instrument rental came with lessons from one of the store's resident instructors. For six weeks I listened earnestly to my instructor and dutifully practiced at home. By the end of that period, I was able to pick out, on my own, the melody of *I Get a Kick Out of You.* At the end of the six week rental period, however, my parents and I were faced with a decision. They could shell out the money to rent the instrument and its accompanying lessons for another six weeks, they could shell out even more to buy an instrument, or I could just give up the sax. My mother and father discussed the costs and benefits of the first two alternatives with me as well as put forth the third option, but they left the decision to me. I could detect, however, from the way they talked, that the cost associated with continuing with the sax would present a financial burden to them, so, to my great regret—which I didn't mention to them—I chose to give up playing it.

While I was still taking sax lessons, I had gotten wind that Norman Granz's *Jazz at the Philharmonic*, an all-star concert hall tour featuring the leading lights of jazz, was playing in Baltimore's Coliseum. The Coliseum was an indoor arena— since demolished—less than a mile from my house. I walked over that night to the arena, where I joined a group of kids from various neighborhoods who had gathered at the back fence outside the hall. We could not see the performers from that vantage point, but we could hear the entire concert.

And at intermission, there they were right in front of us. Several of the players emerged from the stage door to relax, smoke, and talk with one another, right in front of the fence where we were standing. Drummer Gene Krupa, muscular, not very tall, slicked-back hair, and looking quite self assured; Hank Mobley, hard bop tenor saxophonist; Eddie Shu, a guy who seemingly could play any reed instrument; and the great Gerry Mulligan, lanky and boyish-looking baritone sax genius. Having come prepared with index cards, I yelled over the fence asking for their autographs. They all readily complied with my request, with one exception. Gerry Mulligan, ever the cool one, demurred.

"Whaddya want with my autograph, kid?" he asked, fixing me with a stony stare.

"I'm learning to play the sax, Mr. Mulligan," I managed to sputter, "and I would put it inside my sax case to have for all time."

How could Gerry Mulligan resist such a heartfelt request from an aspiring jazz musician? He gave up his autograph to me.

After my Coliseum experience, I came across an ad for a record company that featured only jazz artists. Jazztone Records operated like a mail-order book-of-the-month club. Each month, it sent out a mailer listing several album selections for the month, some of them recorded specifically for the label, others reissued from other labels. I joined the Jazztone Society, as it was called, and each month I could order at my option one or more of its 12-inch, 33-1/3 LP vinyl record albums to be sent to me in the mail. Over the three years the

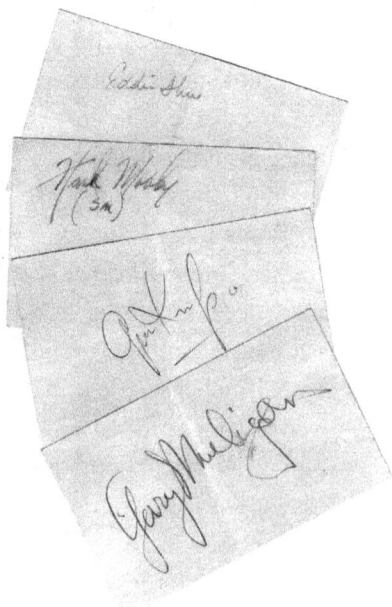

Jazztone Society remained in operation in the United States (it lasted longer in France), I gathered into my record collection almost 50 of its recordings. At first, I went for Dixieland and early jazz albums by artists like Paul Barbarin and his New Orleans Jazz Band, Rex Stewart, Sidney Bechet, Omer Simeon, Jack Teagarden, Jelly Roll Morton, Buck Clayton, and Fats Waller. I got a lot of input and advice from our upstairs tenant, Len Towne, who slowly helped me broaden my interests and tastes to more modern, progressive forms of jazz. Pretty soon, I was adding records of musicians like Charlie Parker, Ruby Braff, Erroll Garner, Stan Getz, Lionel Hampton, Gerry Mulligan, Kai Winding, Chico Hamilton, Bobby Brookmeyer, Zoot Sims, Billie Holiday, Dizzy Gillespie, Coleman Hawkins, and Flip Phillips to my growing collection.

What I liked about the music was that jazz could be sensual, emotional, and visceral or cool, intellectual, and cerebral—or sometimes all of these in the same number. Depending on what I was looking for at the moment, I could find it in jazz. I was hooked on it, and my enthusiasm for it led me to subscribe to *Downbeat* and *Metronome*, magazines read mainly by serious jazz musicians, impresarios, and aficionados. Throughout my high school and college years, I kept up with developments in the jazz scene, particularly with the great jazz saxophonists of the day. I had a favorite for each type of sax: Sidney Bechet, whose soprano sax playing was sweet and melodic; the inimitable Charlie Parker, who could be at once smoothly lyrical and wildly creative on his alto sax; underrated Earl Bostic, whose soaring tenor sax was raunchy and gritty; and, of course, Gerry Mulligan, whose baritone sax playing was cool, vital, and smart. The relative paucity of jazz musicians playing the bass saxophone didn't give me any favorites on that instrument.

To my regret, life after college got to be so busy I could not keep up with music or the field of jazz in as dedicated a fashion as I had before. Nevertheless, in my adult life, I did manage to carve out time to go to see, live, some of the greatest jazz stars of the 20th century, enriching my lifelong appreciation of this American-born musical form. Musicians like Charles Mingus, Marian McPartland, George Shearing, Oscar Peterson, Count Basie (who had played at one of my Senior Week dances at Johns Hopkins), Chuck Mangione, Dave Brubeck, and the Modern Jazz Quartet. There are some that I missed seeing live that I would dearly love to have seen in their heyday, especially Charlie Parker, Ella Fitzgerald, Sarah Vaughan, Billie Holiday, Earl Bostic, and Dizzy Gillespie. Regrettably, they've all passed away. Seeing them in person would really have rounded out my jazz star bucket list.

11

OMG–Not

"Let children learn about different faiths, let them notice their incompatibility, and let them draw their own conclusions about the consequences of that incompatibility.
As for whether they are 'valid,' let them make up their own minds when they are old enough to do so."

— Richard Dawkins, *The God Delusion*

WHEN I WAS growing up on Holmes Avenue, we lived just down the street from the Shaarei Tfiloh synagogue (in Yiddish, the *shul*). This was considered an advantage, as Orthodox Jews are not supposed to create fire on *Shabbos* (the Sabbath)—which driving or riding in a car with its spark plugs firing, turning on lights, or cooking would entail. The congregation's *chazen* (cantor), Jacob Wahrman, lived on Holmes Avenue, too, right across from the *shul*, and our rabbi, Rabbi Nathan Drazin, lived just off the other end of Holmes Avenue in a row house on Auchentroly Terrace—although a somewhat grander one than the Holmes Avenue row houses. Both locations allowed these men to walk to *shul* on *Shabbos* and the other Jewish holidays, as good, observant Orthodox Jews were supposed to do.

While my parents were Orthodox (capital "O") Jews, they were not really orthodox (small "o") Jews. That is, they belonged to the branch of Judaism known as Orthodox Judaism, which is the strictest and most conservative in its practices, but they did not adhere to all of the mandates of Orthodox Judaism as orthodox Orthodox Jews are supposed to do. Yes, Mom *bench licht* (lit candles) every Friday before sundown (when *Shabbos* began), draping a kerchief over her head and saying the accompanying prayer while she lit them; we observed (after a fashion) most of the Jewish holidays; and my parents tried to instill in their children the traditions of Judaism. In many other respects, however, the family did not follow strict Orthodox (capital "O") Jewish practices. We seldom went to *shul* on Shabbos, as was called for; we did not keep a kosher house; we ate non-kosher food such as bacon and crabs; we rode on the Sabbath; and we did not say prayers before every meal or at other prescribed times. I guess you could say we were not strictly Orthodox Jews, nor strictly secular Jews, but somewhere in between.

I don't believe our family was different in most respects from the majority of Jews—all of them Orthodox—in our neighborhood. One of the funniest practices my family engaged in to skirt the Jewish dietary laws centered around eating crabs. Only seafood that has both fins and scales are considered kosher; therefore, crabs are not kosher. But because we lived in the blue point crab capital of the world and crabs are delicious, we ate them anyway. On occasion, Dad would bring home a bagful of steamed crabs. Eating steamed blue point crabs is not a delicate exercise in daintily excising meat from the red-pepper-encrusted shells of the crabs and genteelly placing that meat in one's mouth. No, a crab feast means wooden mallets pounding on the crabs' hard shells, red pepper seasoning flying everywhere, crab feasters tearing out the meat from the cracked claws and bodies of the crabs, then washing it all down with beer (for the adults) or lemonade (for the kids). True Marylanders, we all enjoyed steamed crabs even though they are not kosher.

Because my parents were fearful of being found eating this *tref* (non-kosher) food—who knows, the *chazen* or rabbi could come by at any moment—whenever we had steamed crabs at home, we placed newspapers on the table and the crabs on top of the newspapers. If, god forbid—so to speak—a neighbor, the *chazen*, or the rabbi should ring our doorbell, we could immediately wrap the newspaper up with the crabs inside it, hide the whole mess, wipe the spice off our faces, and act as if we were enjoying a quiet, kosher evening at home. My guess is that 90% of the people in our neighborhood engaged in the same shenanigans as they enjoyed their steamed crabs.

On the Jewish holidays, such as *Succos, Chanukah, Yom Kippur*, and *Rosh Hashanah*, we all got dressed up and walked up the street to *shul*. But the older men in the congregation, many of them from the old country—whichever one it might be—had little tolerance for the fidgets and whispers of the young kids. The old men would punctuate the air with frequent, almost-shouted cries of "Sha!" or dirty looks darted in the direction of any of the young children who rustled in their seats or whispered out of turn. The services also were not particularly interesting to most children, since they were conducted entirely in Hebrew—save for Rabbi Drazin's dry sermons, dryly delivered in English. While the men from the old country were well-versed in Hebrew, most of the young congregants were just learning Hebrew and could not keep up with what was going on in most of the service.

A neighborhood friend of my brother Bill, Dan Levin, recalls the time in 1944 when the International League Baltimore Orioles were on a hot streak, winning everything in sight. As the Little World Series played out during the Jewish High Holidays (*Rosh Hashanah* and *Yom Kippur)*, Levin recalls that "during lulls in the services, there was a mad dash to the firehouse on the corner of Woodbrook and Auchentroly to listen to the games, the firemen in sympathy having placed a tabletop Philco radio outside on a small table."

By the time my friends and I were eight years old or so, our attendance at services during the High Holidays consisted mainly of going outside the building to play on the small area of grass behind it, our *yarmulkes* still perched on our heads. There we would collect chestnuts that had fallen from the trees in Druid Hill Park across the street and play games with them.

Playing on the grass in back of the *shul* facing Auchentroly Terrace subjected us to the occasional forays of Francis Streeters, however. They would travel from their neighborhood up the corridor afforded by the park and stand across the street in the park throwing chestnuts at us while yelling taunts like "Here, you dirty Jews, take this!" We threw chestnuts back at them, an act that was not as brave as it might seem, for we knew the Francis Streeters wouldn't cross Auchentroly Terrace to come onto the *shul* grounds to attack us at closer range and run the risk of bringing out the adults inside to defend their young ones.

Despite the fact that today almost all whites and all Jews have moved out of the neighborhood, the Shaarei Tfiloh synagogue has had such a strong attachment to the hearts of its congregants that it remains, as of this writing, a functioning Jewish congregation in the same location.

I remember the Francis Streeters even now, not so much in fear or rage, but in—what's the best word?—dismay, dismay that one group of humans could have as one of their primary gratifications the hatred of another group of humans. The Francis Streeters may all be gone now, but my dismay about them and other haters remains. Where are you now, Francis Streeters?

The Francis Streeters weren't the only anti-Semites to cross my path. One day after school a bunch of us 2nd-graders were standing on the corner when a girl I knew from school got into an argument with another classmate, Catherine York. It didn't take long for Catherine to excoriate the other girl with "Ah, you dirty Jew" and saunter off. Another time, in high school, I walked with two classmates to a park near our school. Our conversation went on aimlessly the way adolescents' conversations often do. Soon, though, I noticed that Steve Temberbach's talk started to take on a tone meant to impart "otherness" to me, saying things like, "I wonder what *you* people think about that," a sneer and leer appearing simultaneously on his face as he said it. The instances of anti-Semitism I encountered growing up made me immediately sad and fearful, but on reflection I often felt sadder for the person who demonstrated it. I wondered if they knew what they were losing out on by considering a portion of their fellow human beings less than human.

Equally pervasive as the personal instances of anti-Semitism was the institutional anti-Semitism about at the time. New housing developments would brazenly state on their signs and in their printed advertisements "This is a restricted property"— meaning Jews and blacks were not allowed to buy property there. Real estate agents would subtly lead their clients away from Jewish neighborhoods if they were Gentiles and steer Jewish clients only toward Jewish neighborhoods. The residential area abutting The Johns Hopkins University's Homewood campus, Roland Park, remained restricted even into the years that I attended Hopkins.

It's hard to believe now, but even in mid-20th century

America, institutions of higher education had quotas on the number of Jews they admitted. This included, regrettably, my own university. In a book entitled *American Empire: Roosevelt's Geographer and the Prelude to Globalization*, about Isaiah Bowman, the president of Johns Hopkins University from 1935 to 1948, author Neil Smith documented the extent of Bowman's anti-Semitism. Among Bowman's comments and writings, Smith quoted him as commenting in 1939 "there are already too many Jews at Hopkins" and later as worrying that Johns Hopkins was "becoming a practically Jewish organization." In 1942, Bowman instituted a quota on the admission of Jewish students. Happily, my brothers Bill and Leonard made it into Hopkins despite the quota, and I believe that quota was gone by the time I was admitted to Johns Hopkins in the decade that followed theirs.

Medical schools in that era also had quotas on the numbers of Jews they admitted each year. This latter practice ironically led to the widely accepted belief, among both Jews and Gentiles alike, that Jewish physicians were superior because they likely had better qualifications than their non-Jewish counterparts by virtue of having stood out enough from the crowd academically to be among the small number of Jews accepted to medical school in the first place.

I tried not to let any of this personal or societal discrimination affect me greatly. I learned to shy away from sticky situations when confronted by them, all the while feeling a little sorry for myself but sorrier still for those who held these beliefs. Living in a neighborhood that was so heavily Jewish, these kinds of things didn't take up all that much space in my everyday world—at least until I got old enough to start wandering away from my neighborhood.

My parents sent all their children to Hebrew school, as did the parents of most other kids in the neighborhood, hoping to instill

Jewish traditions and practices in us. From the time I was six years old, for two days a week after regular public school, we would go to classrooms in the basement of Shaarei Tfiloh synagogue to be taught the Hebrew language, Jewish history, and religious practices by the likes of Miss Freeman and Mr. Rivkin. I listened to their efforts with one ear, as I think the majority of my Hebrew school classmates did also. Often during Hebrew lessons we cracked jokes and passed around forbidden items to one another. Once, Mr. Rivkin caught Maish Friedman with a loaded water gun we had been passing around. Mr. Rivkin grabbed it from him, and—his face turning a deep crimson and his body nearing a state of apoplexy—threw it to the floor and stomped it into little pieces, plastic and water flying out around the classroom.

I went along with my Hebrew education, growing more and more uninterested in it with each passing year. Strangely, though, I became a "founding member" of the choir of the synagogue. Cantor Wahrman, a patient, placid man, apparently thought he would introduce a modern touch to the congregation by forming a choir of boys to sing at the synagogue services. This was virtually unheard of among the Orthodox congregations I knew of, but that was his goal nonetheless. It wasn't a big choir—only about a dozen boys—but it was still a departure from tradition in that congregation. My motivations for joining this endeavor were that I liked anything musical and I knew some of the other kids who had agreed to be in it. *Chazen* Wahrman got us choir robes, taught us the music and words— Hebrew, of course—and we performed, on occasion, during services.

Herschel Pachino, one of my choir mates, fainted one day during choir practice. It was summer, the *shul* was extremely hot and humid, and, feeling the heat, down he went. After that, Herschel proselytized that we should always wear T-shirts under our choir robes to wick up the sweat, ignoring the ribbing he received from the rest of the choir members about it and his

fainting episode. Although all the other choir members, including me, openly pooh-poohed Herschel's advice, privately it
sounded like a good idea to me, and I made sure to wear a T-
shirt under my robe from then on. And, wouldn't you know, I
didn't faint for any of the time I was in the choir. Which wasn't
very long. For some reason—maybe it was lack of interest or
discipline among the boys, maybe it was resistance from the
congregation at having such a different practice introduced into
the traditional services—the choir lasted only a few months.

Our Hebrew education was meant generally to make us
good, observant Jews, but for boys it was especially meant to
prepare us for Bar Mitzvah, the ritual that confirmed our
passage, in the eyes of the religion, into Jewish adulthood at
the age of 13. I hasten to add here that in my youth, families
did not place such reverence and importance on the similar
ritual for Jewish girls at age 13, Bas Mitzvah, as they do nowadays. This reflected the generally subordinate role of females
in formal Orthodox rituals at the time. Women in an Orthodox
synagogue were expected to sit only in the second floor balcony,
were not expected to participate in the service as fully as men,
and were not as expectantly urged to undergo the rite-of-passage
ritual that Bar Mitzvah was for boys. Things are different now,
but that was then.

As I went through Hebrew school, I thought long and hard
about what I learned there. I tried to imagine what god must be
like and look like, what he did every day, how he could know
what everyone in the world was thinking and doing at every
moment, how to explain his so-called miracles, and how so
many people of so many religions could have so many different
explanations, rationales, and rituals all in the name of the same
deity—and all convinced that theirs was the only way. If there
is but one god, why isn't there but one religion? How could all
the violence, wars, and ills that were brought about throughout
history—the majority of them in the name of, or because of,
religion—be reconciled with the morals and peace espoused

by those religions?

By the time I was 12, I concluded that all religion is bunk. There was no valid and reliable evidence I could see that a divine god exists, or that prayers are answered, or that miracles occur. I decided it is all a delusion understandably clung to by most humans in the face of the smallness they feel confronting the immense forces—war, epidemics, pestilence, death, storms, earthquakes, mountains, vast oceans—and mysteries much larger than themselves. Religious beliefs and rituals, I concluded, were developed by people to give them a sense of comfort in a world that is hard to understand at best and chaotic at worst.

What's more, while religion is touted as being a force for good, my assessment is that the evils done in the name of religion far outweigh the good it is purported to do. It is supposed to be a system that brings people together, but to my mind, it places walls between people more than it brings them together. It is proffered as a philosophy for living, but in my estimation its logic is far overshadowed by its illogicalities.

I didn't mention my non-belief to anyone; I wouldn't unless asked, and I didn't because no one asked. I went through the arduous year-long training for my Bar Mitzvah, learning by heart the Hebrew words and accompanying chant that I would have to sing in front of the whole congregation when my time came to be Bar Mitzvahed, but I did it mainly so as not to disappoint my parents. When the Saturday of my Bar Mitzvah came, I dutifully mounted the *bimah* (dais) wearing a *tallis* (prayer shawl) over the brand new suit bought just for this special occasion and chanted the *haftorah* (the section from the Prophets read on *Shabbos* at the conclusion of the weekly Torah reading) that I had memorized.

After the hour-long ceremony was over, family and friends gathered at our house down the street from the *shul* for a reception my parents had prepared. Many families rented the auditorium in the basement of the *shul* for such a reception, but we couldn't afford to—I was by then, after all, the fourth of the

boys in our family to be Bar Mitzvahed. Mom bought a cake—
at Silber's Bakery, of course—that spelled out "Congratulations
Larry on your Bar Mitzvah" in blue on white frosting, the colors
of the flag of Israel; my sister's fiancé, Lenny, who was an
artist, made a professional-looking sign that echoed the same
sentiment in the same color scheme and hung it on the wall;
and we welcomed my friends and relatives to our house where
they congratulated me profusely. All the while, though, in my
head I knew I was only going through the motions.

After that, I didn't even go through the motions. I did not
attend services, I did not say morning prayers as my oldest
brother Leonard did for as long as he lived at home, and I did
not feel any great interest in Jewish life per se. Yet, in writing
this chapter, I am surprised by how much Jewishness has permeated my life. I guess it boils down to this: Culturally, I am a
Jew, having grown up in a heavily Jewish subculture surrounded
by friends, neighbors, and family who were Jewish. These are
my people, and I am of them. I am an unremitting supporter of

the Jewish homeland that is Israel, the only democratic nation—
and a tiny one at that—amidst a great number of autocratic or
theocratic countries that wish to destroy it. I remain unremittingly appalled at the very idea of the Holocaust and its savage
implementation—the mass shootings, the torture chambers, the
strangling rooms, the sadistic medical experiments, the concentration camps, the gas chambers, and the crematoria. I equally
unremittingly have a visceral distaste for all things German,
even though my head knows that today's Germans and Germany
are not yesterday's Germans and Germany.

As I wrote this book, I was continually surprised at how
much my mind recalled the language, sounds, sights, and smells
of Judaism and the Jewish community I came of age in. And I
admire the Jewish people and culture for their vibrancy, tena-
ciousness, and resilience. Culturally, I am a Jew; religion-wise,
I am an atheist.

12

Sex Rears its Lovely Head

"We are all born sexual creatures, thank God, but it's a pity so
many people despise and crush this natural gift."
— Marilyn Monroe

OKAY, THAT COVERS RELIGION. What other sensitive subjects can I now turn to? Oh, yes, sex. In order to cover that, I have to go back a little before sex.

In my early years, I knew that girls were different from boys, although I wasn't quite certain how. I always was attracted to them because of the mystique they radiated. They seemed softer, livelier, and more enchanting than boys, although it was a mystery to me exactly why they held such charms.

As young as seven years of age, when I went to play with a girl in the neighborhood who was about my age, I tried to find out. It was my idea that we should play doctor. I had no great medical knowledge to impart to her, but our play session imparted to me a knowledge of how girls and boys were differently constructed. I didn't quite know what to do with that information at that age, as no one in my family had filled me in on sex. But the guys around the neighborhood later did, as often with misinformation as with accurate information, in our usual banter. My clandestine reading of "dirty" books and magazines as I got older provided further grist for the mill, as did the occasional "2 by 4" books (crude cartoon books depicting cartoon characters or real people engaging in sexual talk and various sex acts) that we passed from hand to hand. I was an avid learner, and eventually I got the idea. Actual sexual activity was still a way off, however.

As a young adolescent, I went on dates with girls—usually to a movie, party, or dance in her or my neighborhood. Because, at the age of 12, I could not drive, I had to depend on my or the girl's parents to drop us off for our "date" and then pick us up afterward, so there was little chance for much sexual exploration. For a while I went out with Edith Melvin, pretty, *zaftig* (having a full, rounded figure), and nice, but our romantic activities were limited to a goodnight kiss and hug at her door at the end of each date. Ditto for Nancy Zoll, except once, having given the matter considerable advance thought and planning, I slyly put my arm around her as we sat in the dark watching a movie at the Crest Theater. When I let my hand drift down to that beguiling place on girls I had grown to be curious and excited about, her breast, she quietly pushed my hand aside.

My long-term—albeit off-and-on—girlfriend from age 14 to 19 was Quinn Kellner. Once my family moved to Cold Spring Lane, I occasionally visited my cousin Toby, who was a year older than I, at her house a mile away on Reisterstown Road and Cold Spring Lane. Toby ran with a crowd of girls her age who were, on the whole, loud, forward, spunky, and, oh yes, *zaftig*. Among them was Quinn. Like most kids that age, we did a lot of things as a group—went to dances together, parties together, movies together, hung out together. Toby's friends all thought I was "cute" —a major compliment among those girls. They seem to have adopted me as their mascot because of that, and I was the only boy in what we ended up calling "our crowd."

One evening, we were all at Toby's in her parents' bedroom watching television. Several of the girls and I were reclining in a row on the bed watching the program. Toby had made sure that Quinn was placed next to me. I knew Quinn as one of the crowd, and I liked her. I also thought she might like me. As we watched television that night, she took my hand and led it around her shoulder. In a little while, still holding my hand, she guided it down to her breast. It was the most exciting feeling I had experienced in my young life.

After that, I began to see Quinn regularly. She lived near Toby, so I could walk the mile to Quinn's house without much trouble. Quinn was pretty of face, lively, forward, and, like the rest of the girls in our crowd, both a little older than I and *zaftig* (are you beginning to see a pattern here?). We did many things together, and pretty soon we were expressing our puppy love to one another. I asked her to "go steady," which meant seeing each other to the exclusion of anyone else of the opposite sex. Since we were not in the same school—my high school was an all-male one and hers, a coed one—we mainly saw one another on the weekends, when we would go to friends' houses, dances, parties, movies, and local hangouts together as often as we could. Once I reached 16 and obtained a driver's license, we could also park afterwards for some heavy makeout sessions.

Our relationship was volatile, although perhaps no more so than other adolescent relationships. Quinn would often find reason to be unhappy—I think because she felt I was not as committed to her as she was to me—and often that would spark a breakup, with one or both of us ending up in tears. After these occurred, I would be supremely unhappy for weeks at a time, thereby achieving what I imagine, in retrospect, was her objective in breaking up with me. After each such episode, we would eventually find our way back together again.

A year into our relationship, Quinn contracted a serious illness. She was confined to bed for some six months, during which time she could not go to school, and, of course, not go out at all. She bravely told me I should not be limited socially because of this and that we should break up, for my sake. I would have none of that. Puppy love or not, I loved her in that intense way that first love involves, and I refused to agree not to see her anymore. Her malady, though serious, was not contagious, and I tried to visit her every day while she was confined to her bed at home. Often as not, after school I would get off at the bus stop and walk to her house instead of going directly home to mine. On weekends, I would walk to her house to be with her.

As Quinn's condition began to improve, we picked up our physical relationship where we had left off. During one afternoon visit when just she and I were in her family's 2nd floor apartment alone, we were making out pretty intensely as she lay in bed. We lost track of time and were brought out of our reverie with the sound of her mother returning home. Naturally, we quickly broke apart. When Mrs. Kellner came in to her daughter's bedroom, she became alarmed at how flushed Quinn's face was. Quinn and I both backpedaled as quickly and astutely as we knew how, Quinn assuring her mother that she just felt a little hot and feverish but it was nothing to worry about.

The Quinn-Larry relationship went off and on both before and after her recovery, but we still each remained virgins. It was during one of those off times, in my 17th year, that I fell in with Jackie Balanowitz, a girl with a reputation of being "easy." She was about my height, a little older than I, *zaftig*, pretty of face, not overly bright, and who made it clear that she was eager to please. I went out with her a few times. Since I had gotten my driver's license by that time, our dates consisted of my driving the mile and a half to where she lived whenever I could get the car. We would drive around a while, then park on quiet, almost-deserted Cylburn Lane to neck. Our make-out sessions advanced quickly to where it was bare skin upon bare skin.

One day when my mother had gone out with a relative, and I had the car and the house to myself, I phoned Jackie and asked—seeing that I lived near her—if she would like to see where I lived. We both knew it was not the exploration of my digs that was my motivation for the invitation. I picked Jackie up, we drove to my house, and I cursorily showed her around the single floor of my family's living quarters, the tour ending— what a surprise!—in my bedroom. Things advanced quickly from there, and we were soon naked on my bed. And things advanced quickly from there to where we were doing things in bed that I hadn't done before but Jackie surely had.

My parents never talked to me about sex, but then again few parents did discuss the topic in that Eisenhower era of conformity and repression. My brothers and sister had already married and moved out of our house some time before, too. That left me to rely on what I had learned from my buddies to guide me on matters sexual. I recognized that some of their information was misinformation, and I tried to sort it out as best I could. I managed to sort most of it out, and I was careful to take the proper contraceptive/prophylactic precautions.

I went out with Jackie a few more times after that whenever we managed to find an empty spot for our liaisons. After a while, though, my on-again, off-again relationship with Quinn was on again. With Jackie's experience under my belt (literally), I knew now that I could "do it." Further, I thought I was okay at it—Jackie never complained—so I let Quinn know I was experienced. I exaggerated by telling her that I already had had sex with two different girls rather than just one, mainly to make her feel as comfortable as possible and to make myself appear more like a man of the world to her. We both knew we were headed for sex with one another, and with Quinn still being a virgin, I wanted her to feel she was in good hands for her first all-out sexual experience. I think that experience happened in her bedroom when her parents were not home, but I don't recall the exact circumstances now. That is primarily because it was the first of many occasions. We would find whatever ways and means we could to get it on, and in however many ways and means we could think of: in the back seat of the car on deserted lovers' lanes, in her bedroom or living room whenever no one was home there, in my bedroom whenever no one was home there. Quinn was hot for my body and I for hers. It wasn't the only basis for our relationship, but for two hormone-driven adolescents, it provided a foundation for it.

As time went on and my graduation from Johns Hopkins and departure for graduate school loomed, we both began to see the writing on the wall. I was going to be 400 miles away for at least the next four years, and we had both matured psychologically to the extent that we started to realize our young love was based primarily on our physical relationship and that it was likely coming to an end. Quinn was less desirous of seeing it end than I was, but in both of our heart of hearts we knew we were about to go our separate ways. Although she attended my Johns Hopkins University commencement ceremony, and we didn't announce to each other that our relationship was over, when I headed out for Rochester, it was for all intents and purposes goodbye.

After I started graduate school, I sometimes heard about Quinn from my cousin Toby on my occasional trips back home. Eventually, I heard from her that Quinn had married another guy from Baltimore.

Although the end of the story of my amorous exploits in Baltimore does not end the story of my youthful sexual experiences, the rest of those happened after I moved away from home, so that is not grist for this memoir. And further, deponent saith not.

13

LOOKING BACK

"When you think about your past, it's really more in
snapshots. And it jumps around."
— Carmen de Lavallade, co-creator of the dance show *As I Remember It*

A FTER BIDDING Dad good-bye at the side of that road
in Baltimore, I pulled away from him and pulled away
from the life I had known for my first 19 years. I drove toward—
what? A new kind of life, yes, but also the unknown. Would I
survive on my own and become my own person? Would I miss
my family? Would my dreams come true? At that point, I didn't
know the answers, but I knew that the way to find out was to
do what I was doing.

In the intervening years, I came to know some answers.
Not all of them were to my liking, but most were gratifying.
And along the way I learned a few things. To be your own
person, you have to insist on it and not let anyone deter you.
The future may look daunting, you may not always be right,
but you have to stand by your decisions and learn from your
mistakes. To be your own person, you also have to develop a
set of life skills you can feel comfortable with and rely upon.

It's better to choose as your set of life skills and life's work something you like doing, even if you might find more riches doing something you might not like as much. Follow your passion, in other words; it will not only be more fulfilling, your work and your life will be the better for it. I've learned to work hard and get the job done. I'm glad that my upbringing and my heredity gave me the ability to do all that.

To be your own person, you have to set store in toughing out and surviving all the storms and conflicts that may come your way. Survival is all; life is all there is. Don't think there's a better life waiting for you later or that what we have here on this little blue planet is just a rehearsal for some later, better drama. This life here is all there is. There is no second coming, no second chance, no second life. Grab *this* life for all it's worth, hold onto it, and *live* it. It's the only one you'll ever experience.

Don't think that everything happens for a reason. Randomness and luck play a big part. As Richard Dawkins has written in *River Out of Eden*, the universe exhibits "nothing but blind, pitiless indifference." If you are to beat that indifference, you have to set your sights straight and work hard to reach your goals.

I did go on to finish graduate school, earn my doctorate, and become a clinical psychologist who then turned toward conducting research in social science fields that intigued me. I became fairly successful in the public policy consulting company I ultimately worked for for thirty years before retiring as a vice president of that firm. I married a sweet woman, had two absolutely remarkable children—and now, two adorable grandchildren—saw the world, and continued writing.

Of my two parents, Dad died first, in the late 1980s in his late 80s, from a burst thoracic aneurysm. Immediately Mom went into a cognitive and emotional tailspin from which she never recovered. She remained in a vegetative state in a hospital for two years after Dad's death, and then she died, also in her late 80s.

After her death, my oldest brother, Leonard, and his wife went through the family home in Baltimore to sort through all the objects and memories my parents had accumulated over 60 years of marriage. Mom kept photos of the family that she pasted in separate scrapbooks for each of her five children. Len and Elinor sent mine up to me in Massachusetts, along with a few other things Mom and Dad had kept that were connected to me.

One photo in that scrapbook reaches out to me across the years. It's a portrait of me at about two years old that Mom must have had taken by a department store photographer. My hair is deep black, and my eyes are deep blue—it's in black and white, the photograph, but everyone used to remark what blue eyes I had. Everything in that photo looks so fresh and clean, as if to accentuate how bright and innocent and shining everything was then—before I had to wear glasses, make mortgage payments, work for a living. I'm less lively, innocent, and shining now than I was all those years ago. But isn't everyone less lively and innocent and shining as the trials and tribulations and tears and torment and travail of living accumulate? Life has its happinesses, and life has its sadnesses.

How sweet and plain everything was then. I realize that I cannot go back to that time in the photograph when everything was bright and shining, when, above all, the times and I were innocent. Nor do I want or expect to. But I still cherish that photograph that shows the time that used to be. The time before the loss of innocence. The time before my first concrete steps to adulthood.

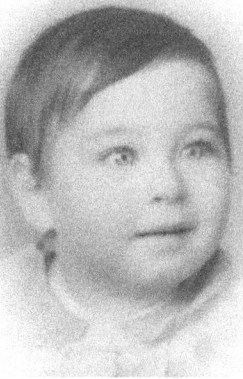

ACKNOWLEDGMENTS

Though writing is mostly a solitary endeavor, no writer does it completely alone. I have many people to thank for helping this memoir reach the point at which it's ready for the wider world to read, although any errors of style or substance are mine, not anyone else's. The written and oral reminiscences of family and friends helped flesh out many of my memories. Early parts of this memoir were tried out at writing workshops in which I participated. Chronologically, they are the Maynard writing group led by Linda Watskin, the Boston-based Grub Street Writers memoir seminar led by Alexandria Marzano-Leznevich, and the memoir workshop led by Nancy Shohet West at her home in Carlisle. I especially thank the participants of the latter group for their incisive critiques of the memoir drafts I shared with them: Lindsay Kafka, Linda McElroy, Catherine Stutz, and, of course, Nancy Shohet West.

Others read and commented on earlier drafts of this book, and I thank them for the time (and courage) to both read and comment on them: Abraham Charrick, Charlie Kerpelman, Margo Melnicove, and Mark Melnicove. They all prompted me about things I might have neglected to include. My brother, Charlie Kerpelman, stands out, not only for his perceptive comments and his help fleshing out incidents and people for which my memories were spotty, but also for being the kind of big brother who served as a role model and mentor for me. Merci, Champ.

I thank Mary Ellen Flaherty, Registrar of The Johns Hopkins University, for researching for me facts and figures about my era as an undergraduate at that excellent institution of higher learning.

Finally, Dixie Coskie led me to Nancy Cleary of MacKenzie-Wyatt Publishing, Inc., who, in turn, helped me ready my manuscript for publication.

If there are others who helped me bring this project to fruition whom I have forgotten to mention, please accept my apologies.

Larry C. Kerpelman

ABOUT THE AUTHOR

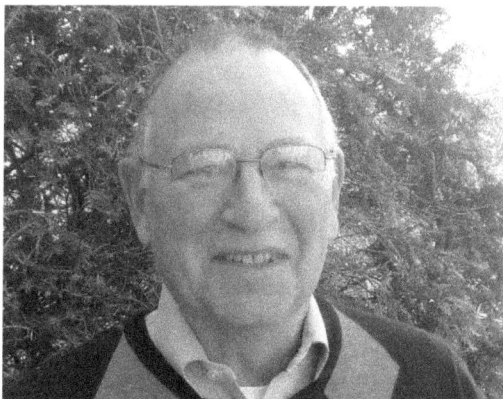

Larry C. Kerpelman's career has encompassed clinical work, teaching, research, and writing. His writing has appeared in popular, academic, and medical publications worldwide. One reviewer called his 2011 book *Pieces Missing: A Family's Journey of Recovery from Traumatic Brain Injury* "at once both inspiring and informative." His story "Joanie" was published in the 2014 anthology *Chicken Soup for the Soul: Recovering from Traumatic Brain Injury*. He lives in Massachusetts with his wife Joanie, and he continues to write about matters that intrigue him.

Read more about him at www.LCKerpelman.com.

www.ingramcontent.com/pod-product-compliance
Lightning Source LLC
Chambersburg PA
CBHW031150020426
42333CB00013B/603